REFRAMING FINANCE

REFRAMING FINANCE

New Models of Long-Term Investment Management

Ashby Monk, Rajiv Sharma,
Duncan L. Sinclair

BLOOMSBURY
NEW DELHI • LONDON • OXFORD • NEW YORK • SYDNEY

BLOOMSBURY INDIA
Bloomsbury Publishing India Pvt. Ltd
Second Floor, LSC Building No. 4, DDA Complex,
Pocket C – 6 & 7, Vasant Kunj,
New Delhi 110070

BLOOMSBURY, BLOOMSBURY INDIA and the Diana logo are
trademarks of Bloomsbury Publishing Plc

First published in the United States of America by Stanford University Press 2017
First published in India 2022

ISBN: 978-93-54358-53-1
2 4 6 8 10 9 7 5 3 1

For sale in the Indian subcontinent only

Typeset by Newgen in 10/14 Minion
Printed and bound in India by Replika Press Pvt. Ltd.

To Courtney, Henry, and Beatrix

To Mum, Dad, and Avinash

To Michelle Sinclair and Joshua Unrau

Contents

Figures and Tables

Figures

Tables

Preface and Acknowledgments

THE OBJECTIVE IN WRITING THIS BOOK was to tie together some of the research we have been conducting at our research center at Stanford University, which looks at understanding how the largest sources of investment capital in the world can be channeled into projects that address some of the most pressing challenges in the world, such as solutions to climate change or the development of new infrastructure. We sit in the Civil and Environmental Engineering Department at Stanford, which may appear strange. It isn't. We work with the engineers walking the hallways to help them think creatively about their own projects and where to look to find aligned financial partners that can maximize their chances for success.

In our view, if the financing doesn't come together in the right way, the projects being undertaken may not be successful even if the ideas are sound and the execution solid. For example, if an engineer wants to develop a new type of green building that has a sophisticated energy conservation component, this engineer will likely want long-term investors involved right from the beginning. Why? Because the terminal investors will reap much of the value from the energy cost reductions associated with the investment in efficiency. Trying to cobble together short-term financing with leverage to fund these long-term projects would be inefficient, risky, and expensive in terms of the layering of fees and costs. Intuitively, it doesn't make sense. Large, long-term projects need large, long-term investors. That's where we come in.

In short, through our work at Stanford's Global Projects Center, we're trying to fix finance for the people thinking big thoughts about infrastructure, real estate, computer science, water, energy, and so on.

At the core of our finance problem is the current capitalist system. The key building block of this system is the large asset owner investors that provide much of the capital that drives companies and organizations around the world. This book contributes to ushering in a new dawn of finance-led capitalism that demands that the global community of long-term asset owners—endowments, family offices, insurance companies, pensions, and sovereign funds—be more professional and invest in long-term assets such as infrastructure, private equity, real estate, timber, and agriculture. The idea is for the ultimate principals in the long principal-agent chain of intermediaries—a chain that facilitates the flow of resources between savers and developers in our capitalist system—to take on more responsibility than they have previously and find more-aligned partnership-based vehicles for long-term investment.

We adopt geographic, economic, sociological, and organizational management frameworks to address the problems of long-term investment. Central to this is the use of social network theory to understand the significance of the actors that sit in the middle of the savings-investment channel. We then illustrate the importance of social capital for an institutional investor organization to help build organizational capacity and move as far along the spectrum as possible toward directly investing in long-term assets. Relational contract theory, which has its foundations rooted in economic sociology, also provides guidance on how more alignment can be achieved between investors and their financial service providers.

This theoretical underpinning provides the validation of a new model of institutional investment that we call "the collaborative model of long-term investment." Such a model can be compared with the other distinct models that seem to have emerged in the world of institutional investment management. The Norway model, based on the practices of the country's sovereign wealth fund, is characterized by following a low-cost passive investing framework in public-market securities. Public-market benchmarks are used and there is the belief that markets are largely efficient. This is an older model that a number of funds use today. A newer model is the endowment model formulated by David Swenson, chief investment officer of the Yale University endowment. The endowment model is based on allocating assets to alternative asset classes such as private equity, hedge funds, and real estate through external managers. Because the endowment model is completely outsourced, the internal team is small and significantly higher costs are associated with this strategy. The third model to emerge is the Canadian model, which, like the endowment model, is based on investing in alternative asset classes but differentiates itself by the fact that it is largely in-sourced and requires hiring expert internal staff to carry out most of the investment function. There are pros and cons of each investing model, and investors have incorporated aspects of each into their overall portfolio construction.

We believe the collaborative or partnership-based model of investing is the latest model of institutional investment to emerge. This model focuses on channeling institutional investor capital into the long-term private-market asset classes of infrastructure, real estate, clean energy, private equity, agriculture, and timber; that is, the real economy. The distinguishing characteristic of the collaborative model is that it is based on new co-investment partnerships among peer investors, joint ventures with specific developers or management teams, and redefined aligned relationships with external managers with the aim of getting as close to the underlying investments as possible. The collaborative model is new. The vehicles that have the distinguishing characteristics of the model have in large part been set up only in the last few years. This book conceptualizes and validates why and how these vehicles are being created and the implications that this will have on the industry.

The empirical evidence we draw on in our examination of the collaborative model is of two main types. The first is semistructured formal and informal interviews with asset owner organizations, asset managers, and other intermediaries in the investment management process. Altogether, we have conducted over 100 such interviews to inform our thoughts, mainly in the United States, Canada, the United Kingdom, South Africa, France, Singapore, India, Australia, and New Zealand over the last five years.

The second form of research we have employed is participant observation in both formal and informal capacities. All authors have worked in the major organizations that have formally instigated long-term investing roundtable and think-tank initiatives (as per Chapter 2). On top of this, the authors have been involved in the formal setup of two peer-led co-investment platforms in the clean-energy space. In addition, we also draw occasionally on the personal experiences of the authors in their capacity as institutional investor advisors and in their previous working lives in investment management.

Quantitative information on strategies and networks for institutional investors is not publicly available, which limits the type of analysis carried out. Because the collaborative model of investment is new, not much data is available to assess the performance of the vehicles yet. Therefore we seek to understand the lessons learned in the setup and development of the initiatives. We believe the data limitations are not sufficient to devalue the methods used in this book. The book is intended to be illustrative and to provide a useful guide for institutional investors, scholars, and other commentators who work within the bounds of the theoretical and practical topics discussed.

We need to thank many people who helped make this project possible. First, we would like to acknowledge the direct support of Stanford University's Global Projects Center and the members of the research consortium on institutional investment. Members of the research consortium provided access, field assistance, and financial support throughout this project, though members were not involved in the formation of the book's content and argument. In particular, we would like to thank Jagdeep Bachher, Scott Kalb, Adrian Orr, Nigel Gormly, and Ray Levitt for their feedback on the work throughout. A special dedication should go to Christian Racicot and the Quebec City Conference for their support. We would also like to thank Wen Feng for his research assistance in Chapter 2 and to Grant Duhamel for his help in collating the collaborative vehicles database.

We are grateful for the mentorship of Gordon L. Clark. Gordon in many ways inspired our initial interest in the topic of asset owners and institutional investment. He has continued to provide support, feedback, and critique of our work throughout this project.

Outside academia, we have benefited immensely from the exposure we have gained by working with various institutions in industry in formal employment and consulting capacities. We appreciate the time and conversations with colleagues at the following institutions that have helped shape our thoughts: Alberta Investment Management Corporation, University of California Office of the CIO, Australian Super, First State Super, New Zealand Superannuation Fund, Deloitte Canada, Institutional Investors Roundtable, Sovereign Investor Institute, OECD, Ministry of Finance of Sweden, and Institutional Investor Euromoney.

REFRAMING FINANCE

1 A Collaborative Model for Long-Term Investing

"The single most realistic and effective way to move forward is to change the investment strategies and approaches of the players who form the cornerstone of our capitalist system: the big asset owners . . . If they adopt investment strategies aimed at maximizing long-term results, then other key players—asset managers, corporate boards and company executives—will likely follow suit."

THIS QUOTE BY MCKINSEY & CO. global managing partner Dominic Barton and Canada Pension Plan Investment Board CEO Mark Wiseman encapsulates what this book seeks to achieve. We focus our attention on the building blocks of the capitalist system, the large-asset owner-investors, and examine how they can more positively impact their own fiduciaries as well as the wider economy and society.

With the global population expected to increase to ten billion by 2050 and the proportion of people living in cities expected to double, the strain that this will place on existing infrastructure, housing requirements, farmland, and other natural resources will be profound. In order to avoid the effects of irreversible climate change, deepening inequality, and even military conflicts over resources, we will need to unlock large pools of long-term capital to fund resource and infrastructure innovation. We classify long-term investments[1] as investments in illiquid, private-market asset classes such as infrastructure, clean energy, real estate, venture capital, agriculture, timber, and private equity that can produce attractive financial returns and, by their nature, can have significant impacts in the economy and wider society.

It is critically important for the health of our capitalist system and indeed the world that the global community of long-term investors begin investing in long-term projects that will help address our global challenges and prepare us for this future state. According to the Organisation for Economic

Co-operation and Development (OECD), the community of long-term investors has more than $100 trillion in assets under management,[2] which means there should be plenty of capital available for the costly economic transitions ahead.

The significance of long-term investing for large institutions has risen to prominence after the drawbacks of short-termism and myopic behavior were exposed in the financial crisis of 2008–2009. The crisis highlighted badly misaligned economic incentives; the poor performance of highly leveraged, complex financial institutions; and a lack of value-add from the short-term-oriented financial services sector. Financial regulation since has attempted to provide reform for long-term stability and restore discipline in the market place. Such changes in behavior are crucial for megabanks but also for the largest holders of capital, typically asset owner institutional investors located around the world.

So who are these long-term investors and what are their characteristics? Institutional investors or asset owners[3] such as sovereign wealth funds, endowments, foundations, family offices, pension funds, and life insurance companies have long-term profiles and can be separated from mutual funds, private-equity firms, and other asset management firms that invest on behalf of the institutional investors, sometimes criticized for their more short-term-oriented behavior. *Sovereign wealth funds* (SWFs) are institutional investors set up by governments and are usually funded by budget surpluses to provide long-term benefits to a nation.[4] *Pension funds* provide retirement payments for pension scheme members and consist of either defined-benefit or defined-contribution systems. Defined-benefit plans are required to pay a certain amount to their beneficiaries at a certain time in the future. Defined-contribution plans, instead, are based on contributions and the performance of investments to generate a retirement annuity for plan beneficiaries. *Life insurance companies* are considered long-term investors because of their requirements to pay beneficiaries or policyholders in the future. *Endowments/foundations* are used to fund the expenses of nonprofit organizations and generally have a mandate to exist in perpetuity, providing a steady stream of income to their beneficiaries. Finally, *family offices* manage the wealth of high-net-worth families and have the mandate to manage wealth for future generations of family members, requiring a long-term outlook for investments.[5]

Sadly, even with the large amounts of long-term capital available, the mobilization of long-term investors (LTIs) toward long-term projects is not happening. We still have widening gaps in infrastructure and energy innovation financing. The patient investors needed to support the capital-intense, long-development ventures and projects that could, for example, reduce greenhouse gas emissions at scale simply are not there. We recognize that it is not an investor's job to solve climate change or fix our infrastructure, but it is the fiduciary obligation of a pension fund or endowment to maximize financial returns. Investing in these long-term projects in the right way has shown to be financially rewarding.[6] There may be an abundance of LTIs, but for a variety of reasons, most LTIs are not exercising their long horizon.

This is partly because the investment management process involves many parties and intermediaries, such as asset managers, placement agents, and consultants. These intermediaries provide expertise in information gathering and scale advantages in investment costs. However, the multiple layers of intermediation can also create agency conflicts and misalignment of objectives. If institutional investors delegate the asset management to intermediaries in order to shift responsibility and reduce perceived risk, they then violate their fiduciary duty and may not be acting in the best interest of their beneficiaries.[7]

In the case of infrastructure, the situation is quite paradoxical. Most governments around the world are sitting on a large backlog of infrastructure projects that they are unable to fund effectively. And yet the same governments are also often in control of large pools of pension or sovereign assets that they struggle to invest effectively. Clearly, there are bottleneck issues around the way in which the largest long-term sources of capital in the world are intermediated with the long-term projects that are most in need of investment. A lot of the funding has to come from "off-balance-sheet" transactions for these governments, as many do not have the capability to fund the projects because of already high debt levels. While pension funds and sovereign funds have a primary commercial objective, we argue that their long-term characteristics make them more amenable to achieving wider long-term economic and social goals, compared with short-term-oriented, opportunistic types of investors such as certain asset management firms. On top of this, if pension funds and sovereign funds do achieve their long-term financial objectives, it is likely that these benefits will accrue back to the citizens of governments that need the funding. This book tries to address how more of these benefits can be enjoyed by asset owners rather than be disproportionately swallowed up by opportunistic financial intermediary firms.

There is ample academic and empirical evidence to show that institutional investors that are able to invest directly into private assets can outperform those that delegate their asset management function to external intermediaries.[8] There is also evidence to suggest that allocations to private-market assets can have significant benefits to institutional investors.[9] As a result, many investors are looking to increase their allocations to private markets. Given these trends in the industry, this book looks at how institutional investors can access private-market assets in the most efficient way possible. In essence, the book argues for and provides the premise for the *collaborative model of institutional investment*. Such a model is based on institutional investors developing an efficient and effective network to form long-term relationships with trusted investment partners. The collaborative or partnership-based model of institutional investment combines aspects of the Canadian direct investing model and the David Swensen–pioneered endowment model of investing in private market assets[10] with some new collaborative mechanisms and strategies. This is depicted in Figure 1.1. We use the term *re-intermediation* to explain the rationale behind the collaborative model of long-term investing. Three main components to the re-intermediation thesis are proposed here:

First, as has been mentioned (and backed up by the literature), institutional investors that can in-source investment management services and make direct investments should do so. The universe of direct investors has been increasing steadily as a result of greater inflows of assets and the realization that their process can be more efficient.

Second, while financial intermediaries have gained excessively in the past at the expense of many institutional investors, the financial services industry has been established for a significant period of time, and substantial value has been created by a number of these organizations providing the services of fund placement, asset management, consulting, and advising. As Warren (2014) states: "the asset management industry has been a source of economic growth, as a valuable intermediary in the savings-investment channel." The second aspect of the re-intermediation thesis is thus focused on constructive engagement with intermediaries. Investors that cannot invest directly should engage with intermediaries in a novel way to ensure that the interests of asset owners are more aligned with those facilitating the deployment of capital. Specifically, this alludes to asset managers, fund of funds, consultants, and placement agents restructuring their business models to ensure that they are

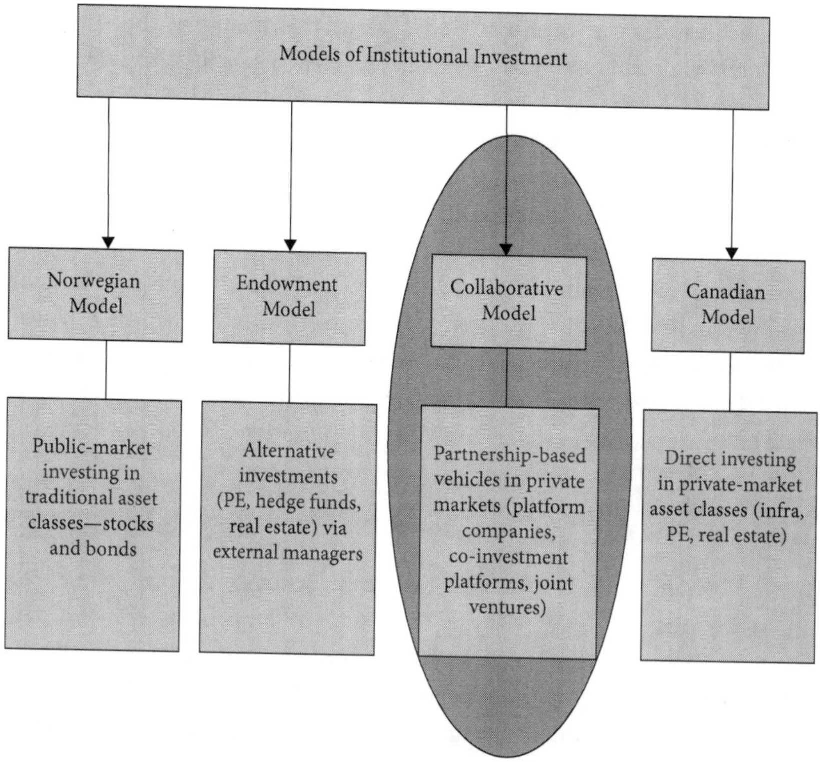

FIGURE 1.1 The collaborative model of long-term investing

adding real value to the investment management process in a transparent, honest way.

Third, co-investments made by specific-purpose vehicles or platforms where peer investors come together to invest is also part of the re-intermediation process. The idea here is to bring like-minded investors together in a club or joint venture arrangement with a specific mandate to invest collaboratively into certain assets. Although some sophistication would be required among co-investors to be a part of such a vehicle, these initiatives may allow slightly smaller investors to gain access to private-market deals in a much more aligned way than through the fund manager route.

Central to the re-intermediation thesis is the need for investors to form an effective, efficient network to facilitate investments into the information-ally opaque private-market asset classes. This involves developing strong relationships with peer investors as well as with intermediaries and other parties to form aligned investment partnerships that help achieve the objectives of the investment management process. In order to analyze these interorganizational dynamics at play, we draw on sociology theory to support the arguments in this book.

While the intention here is not to be an academic textbook, we use economic sociology theory to illustrate the importance of investors building their network. Economic sociology theory is also used to inform investors of how a more relational, transparent form of governance can be achieved with their intermediaries. We then provide case studies of how innovative partnership-based vehicles are being set up by institutional investors to illustrate how investors can get closer to the assets of interest.

The Value of Long-Term Investing

Institutional investors that exercise their long-term investing capabilities can add significant value to society and the wider economy. Long-term investors can have positive influences on individual businesses by realizing long-term value creation and improving their longer-term prospects. Theoretically, they can provide liquidity during critical times and help stabilize financial markets. When acting in a long-term manner, they are not prone to herd mentality and can retain assets in their portfolios in times of crisis, and in this way play a countercyclical role.

While this book is predominantly focused on private-market investing, the drawbacks of short-termism for an institutional investor can be seen through the returns of the U.S. stock market. As indicated in Figure 1.2, the S&P 500 since 1970 has grown in value a hundred times over. However, between 2000 and the end of 2009, the return of the market was in fact negative (–0.3% nominal, –3.0% real). An investor that held stocks for the whole period compared with just between 2000 and 2009 would have reaped significant benefits.

Figure 1.3 illustrates how short-termism has crept into the investment decision-making process for investors with the average holding period of stocks declining significantly over the last 50 years. This is true for most stock indices around the world:[11]

The Harvard Management Company (HMC), which is responsible for the investment of Harvard University's endowment fund, illustrated how

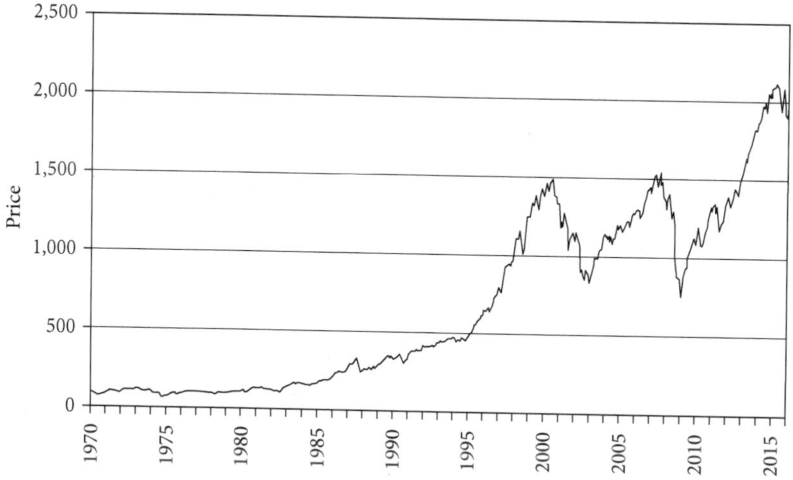

FIGURE 1.2 Performance of S&P 500 since 1970
SOURCE: S&P via Yahoo! Finance.

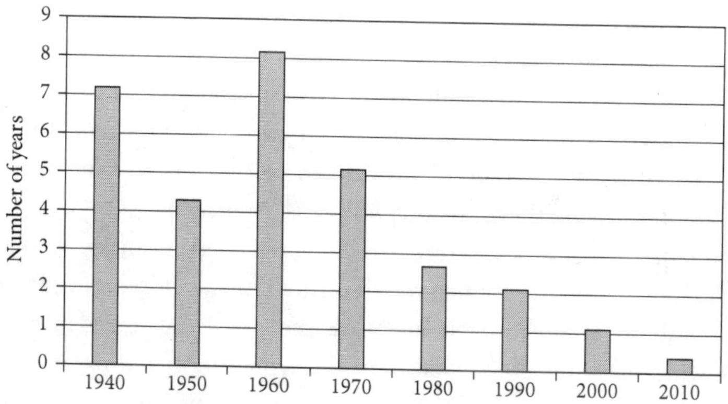

FIGURE 1.3 Average holding period for stocks by decade
SOURCE: LPL Financial, New York Stock Exchange (NYSE).

institutional investors can be crippled by short-termism. In the 2008–2009 financial crisis, because of the lockup of its capital in risky derivative instruments offered by external asset managers, HMC faced a liquidity crisis to cover its operating budget. As a result, HMC was forced to sell a number of its stakes in illiquid asset classes at large discounts, resulting in large losses for the endowment. In this way, HMC suffered as a result of not taking advantage of its position as a long-term investor to reduce the effects of cyclical downturns.[12]

Investors with a long-term perspective stand to make better returns by accessing risk premia, taking advantage of macroeconomic trends, influencing better corporate governance, avoiding buying high and selling low, and minimizing transaction costs.[13] Long-term investors are more able to buy assets at distressed prices during market dislocations and to access asset classes and investments closed to investors with more limited time horizons. The potential for higher returns has benefits for long-term savings and pension funds, thus alleviating some of the funding gap that is widening because of low interest rates and an increased demographic burden. Beneficiaries of institutions and general taxpayers stand to benefit from the implementation of long-term investment strategies. In the economic environment following the 2008–2009 financial crisis, characterized by low yields, mounting volatility, low global economic growth, and below-average investment returns, the contrast between short-term transaction-oriented markets and opportunities in long-term nonpublic assets such as real estate, infrastructure, and private equity has been particularly accentuated.[14]

The OECD summarizes the importance of long-term investors in three ways: they provide patient capital that yields higher net investment rates of return by taking advantage of illiquidity premia and lowering turnover; they provide engaged capital that promotes better corporate governance as shareholders are encouraged to adopt ongoing and more direct roles in investment strategies; and finally they provide productive capital that supports sustainable growth, such as infrastructure development and green energy, and fosters competitiveness and economic growth.[15] In contrast, short-termism undermines the ability of companies to invest and grow, with the missed investments having wider-reaching consequences in the economy, including slower GDP growth, higher unemployment, and lower return on investment for savers.[16]

We are not the first to posit that large institutional investors can make an important contribution to growth, in particular through financing long-term projects, such as infrastructure, clean technology, real estate, and agriculture.[17] Infrastructure in particular has been the subject of much attention for attracting long-term investment, as most nations around the world struggle to address their infrastructure investment deficits. Infrastructure provides significant benefits by contributing to economic growth, which further emphasizes the value of long-term investors in these assets.[18]

Infrastructure services are physical facilities that provide the building blocks of a functioning society. Within this broad concept, social infrastructure (e.g., health and education) can be distinguished from economic infrastructure. Economic infrastructure relates to the channels, pipes, conduits, and apparatus that deliver power and water, provide protection from floods, and take away waste. It also includes the roads, railways, airports, and harbors that allow the safe movement of people and goods between communities. These services directly support the well-being of households as well as production activities of enterprises at various points of the value chain and are thus directly relevant to the competitiveness of firms and to economic development.[19]

Specifically, the power industry, comprising generation, transmission, and distribution, forms an integral part of the backbone of a modern economy. Without adequate investment and a reliable supply of power, an economy is unable to function efficiently, and economic growth targets are difficult to achieve because of outages and blackouts. An integrated transport infrastructure that includes roads, railways, airports, and seaports makes it possible to link underdeveloped areas into the global economy. Investments in transport infrastructure allow goods and services to be transported more quickly and at lower cost, resulting in both lower prices for consumers and increased profitability for firms. Water infrastructure relates to the delivery, treatment, supply, and distribution of water to its users as well as the collection, removal, treatment, and disposal of sewage and wastewater. Investment in water infrastructure is crucial for sustaining the central role that it plays in human societies while also protecting aquatic ecosystems, which is critical for the environment.[20]

A number of studies have shown the relationship between infrastructure investment and economic growth. Most of the research in this area has been based on the production function approach, where output elasticity with respect to public capital (regarded as a synonym for infrastructure) is calculated to determine whether higher rates of government expenditure can increase long-run growth rates.[21] Early work indicated that a positive relationship exists between private-sector output and infrastructure investment.[22] The direction of causality and quality of data were highlighted as limitations of the early studies; nevertheless, further work has also shown a positive relationship between public capital and private output.[23] Using an annual time-series growth regression, Égert and colleagues (2009) provide additional evidence showing that the contributions of infrastructure have a positive impact on economic growth.

Investments in other private-market asset classes can also be seen to have wider economic impacts. Venture capital investments that back entrepreneurs and new businesses, for example, have been proven to contribute to economic development.[24] The businesses that benefit from venture capital financing can result in new employment and the stimulation of related businesses or sectors that support a new venture. Through unique offerings of new goods and services and production processes, entrepreneurs can improve efficiency, and innovation leads to economic growth.[25]

Similarly, certain real estate development investments have provided economic benefit, particularly those in underdeveloped areas, which could be classed as targeted investments.[26] In fact, institutional investors that have had a specific development focus on investing in real estate, private businesses, and infrastructure have been able to post attractive investment returns.[27]

By 2030, as global population surpasses eight billion, there will be significant increases in food demand, placing pressure on agricultural crops. Investments in agriculture seem to be suited to LTIs and necessary for improving output productivity to meet global demand. The growing middle class in the developing world will be looking to consume more and more protein. A shift toward greater global protein consumption will increase demand for grain dramatically. On top of this, continued development and industrialization will reduce the land resources for agriculture. All of these long-term economic factors will drive the value of agriculture assets, highlighting the attraction for long-term investors in this area.[28]

Clean-technology companies that help mitigate climate change require significant amounts of financing and should be ideally suited to long-term institutional investors. In the past, in order to access green energy opportunities, investors would normally seek out a third-party asset manager to do an inventory of the investible assets and make investment decisions. But the scale and time horizon of these companies do not often fit within the fund structures of existing intermediaries, which is partly why so few investors made attractive returns in this sector over the past decade. In our view, the best sources of capital for clean-technology companies are more often than not LTIs. LTIs have intergenerational time horizons and deep pockets, which makes them valuable partners for capital-intensive and long-gestation companies. In this way, by leveraging off their key attributes (scale and time horizon), institutional investors stand to make attractive returns and have significant impact.

Barriers to Long-Term Investment

Despite the many benefits and advantages of institutional investors investing in long-term private-market assets, not only to achieve greater returns but for the wider economy, a number of other intrinsic constraints inhibit the flow of capital. The extent of each constraint for long-term investment will depend on the type of investor. There are also general behavioral theories and explanations for why short-termism may creep into the investment decision-making process of institutional investors. Structural factors may make it difficult to implement some of the ideas from this book. The objective, however, is to educate the reader on how novel methods are being developed to address some of the challenges and how the industry may be shaped in the future.

The first key constraint that may affect the investment time horizon of an institutional investor is their *liability* profile. Institutional investors that need to make payouts in the near term may not be able to invest in illiquid investments that have long lockup periods. They may not be able to take on short-term volatility, which prohibits them from holding assets over the long-term. Pension funds, endowments, and foundations have a proportion of their current asset base that needs to be distributed over a given time period. Family offices and sovereign wealth funds have minimal short-term liabilities and can therefore afford to devote a larger proportion of their assets to long-term assets. The types of liabilities are summarized in Table 1.1.

Related to the liability constraint is that of funding risk. An ongoing focus on funding ratios or capital adequacy may induce a short horizon, even though the funding is secure or the liability is relatively predictable. An example of this occurred when the Harvard endowment fund suffered because of an unanticipated need to sell illiquid assets to meet cash flow needs during the global financial crisis (GFC). An investor who acknowledges that they may be forced into selling positions at short notice may be reluctant to take

TABLE 1.1 Types of investor liabilities

Types of liabilities	*Types of investor*
Defined or fixed-obligation liabilities	Insurers, pension funds
Defined proportion of total pool of assets per annum	Foundations, university endowments
Flexible liabilities not mandatory to be fulfilled each year	Family offices, sovereign wealth funds

SOURCE: WEF 2011.

long-term positions, especially in illiquid assets that they cannot readily exit in the event of redemptions.

Another consideration is whether an institutional investor is facing net inflows or net outflows from their fund. Investors will be more confident that they will not be placed in the position of needing to sell into weak markets if they are confident that they will continue to draw inflows. Using data from 152 large superannuation funds in Australia during 2004–2010, Cummings and Ellis (2015) provide evidence that fund flows influence the weightings held in illiquid assets. In particular, although the authors note that the heterogeneous nature of funds makes correlations difficult, they deduced that larger funds with larger positive fund flows have a larger weighting to illiquid assets.

The *risk appetite* of an institution depends on a number of restrictions and will determine whether a long-term investment strategy will be employed. A long-term institutional investor should be willing to accept moderate levels of risk, short-term volatility, and potential permanent capital loss and not divest from long-term investments in the face of market pressure.[29] However, investors that have defined liabilities are often heavily regulated, which affects their risk profiles and how risky assets are treated in their accounts. Some regulators require investors to hold high capital ratios if investments are made into illiquid investments, which influences them to invest in low-risk assets. The pressure faced by asset owners to maintain funded status in the short term and report to the market on a short-term basis results in many investors having a low-risk appetite.

Other types of stakeholders may also put pressure on long-term institutions and influence their risk appetite. Large public pension funds and sovereign wealth funds may be subject to the opinions of politicians who may feel alarmed whenever volatility in asset prices leads to a dramatic fall in a fund's value, regardless of whether that volatility had been taken into account. This type of pressure will make certain investors cautious about making the investments in the first place. Similarly, endowments and foundations face pressure from their trustees to perform in the short term, with operating budgets for certain institutions coming from their funds. When short-term gains are made, this often leads to an increase in spending, making it difficult to invest for the long term.[30]

The investment *decision-making process* within an institutional investor organization may also provide constraints for the implementation of a long-term investment strategy. Social structures within firms and groupthink can contribute to an organization's reluctance to adopt a long-term view.[31]

Investment managers are often incentivized to maximize their performance over the short term, in line with bonus and other compensation payouts, or their performance may be pegged to an index benchmark such as the S&P 500, discouraging investment decisions to be made over the long term with different performance trajectory to the benchmark employed.[32]

Another important consideration is the length of the decision chain from the principal to the ultimate deployer of capital. Kay (2012) suggests that this chain creates misalignments such as bias for action, as agents aim to justify their positions. The longer the decision chain, the higher the prospect of misalignment and the higher the cost of investments. The principal agent issues between asset owners and managers is a key motivation behind this book. The problem is further addressed later in this chapter. Chapter 3 on re-intermediating managers also returns to the subject and attempts to provide solutions.

• • •

Behavioral and psychological issues have also been attributed to the short-term tendencies of investment institutions.[33] Academic research in biology and neuroeconomics has shown that emotional and cognitive processes interact and affect the ability to make decisions for the long or short term. These studies indicate that a preference for immediate consumption may have emerged as a survival strategy.[34] Similarly, desire for immediate gratification has been found to be stronger when rewards are more salient.[35]

Atherton and colleagues (2007) highlight the role of accepted behaviors and norms such as the materialistic society we live in, which demands immediate returns and satisfaction. This can drive short-termism and is seen as the accepted way of doing things, creating peer pressure to conform.

Long-term investing requires a certain amount of *resource capability* to address the unique types of risks that are played out over a longer time frame. Certain institutional investors face budget pressures that prevent them from acquiring the necessary research tools and internal expertise to help execute a long-term investment strategy. The market for investing talent is highly competitive, and there are considerable challenges in attracting the necessary expertise because of restricted compensation levels and relatively fewer staff in organizations such as public-sector pension funds and sovereign wealth funds.

Quite often the size of assets of a fund dictates not only the governance and internal capability to evaluate investments but also an institution's access to opportunities. As a result, smaller institutional investors tend to have more conservative asset allocations compared with the largest institutional investors.

The average tenure of a chief investment officer is approximately four years, meaning that long-term investing can provide a significant career risk.[36] The tenure for more junior staff may be shorter and there can be significant pressure to perform within this period to achieve career progression. As a result, assets with a short time frame may be more attractive to invest into.[37]

There may also be constraints to long-term investment by institutional investors due to implicit understandings about the market and where the highest returns can be achieved. Long-term investment requires the belief within institutions that the returns generated from making long-term investments will be large enough to justify the associated risks, such as liquidity risk. Within an institutional investor organization, principals, trustees, and managers must believe strongly in a long-term investment strategy and understand counterarguments before investments can be made.

Long-Term Investment Constraints: U.S. Public Pension Funds as an Example

The U.S. defined-benefit public pension fund sector has been regarded as an institutional investor model that is based on politicized and underresourced investment operations. Pension funds in the United States are predominantly the result of government policy makers and have grown in size to over $22 trillion in 2014.[38] Pension funds in the United States are heavily constrained by policies that affect the risk appetite and decision-making capability of the investment professionals that populate these organizations. In government agencies, there are restrictions on the compensation levels of employees, which has led to a huge reliance on the asset management industry. The trend in the United States has been to limit the direct costs of managing the pension, thus reducing salary and head count, instead of reducing fees paid to asset managers, which are more directly tied to performance and in many cases more difficult to measure. For example, the largest pension fund in the country, the California Public Employees' Retirement System (CalPERS), paid $1.6 billion in management fees in 2014 to external managers.

The average analyst salary in a U.S. public pension fund is $90,000 (a factor of 3 or 4 less than in the private asset management industry), and a team of two to four people could be responsible for a multibillion-dollar allocation.

As a result of the way the system has been formed, a number of principal-agent issues have arisen between U.S. pension funds and their asset managers. For example, the Securities and Exchange Commission (SEC) has been investigating 400 private-equity General Partners (GPs) and found that "a majority of private equity firms inflate fees and expenses charged to companies in which they hold stakes."[39] Similarly, on the asset owner side, major public pension funds in the United States have recently admitted that they do not track hundreds of millions in fees paid to asset managers.[40]

Many U.S. public pension funds require board approval before certain investments can be made. Board members of a public pension are usually elected representatives of the fiduciary body and not investment professionals. Quite often, the board of a pension fund is also the investment committee, and so investment decisions will need to be agreed upon by the committee before capital can be deployed. This can severely restrict a pension fund from making investments opportunistically into attractive long-term assets. For certain assets like infrastructure that are politically sensitive, gaining approval from the board may be difficult if there are political issues such as labor union effects with privatized infrastructure.

While the liability structure for each fund will be different, the pension crisis in the United States and in many other countries has placed a greater emphasis on sound long-term investment strategies to help fund the increasing deficit between workers in the economy and pensioners retiring. Pension funds need to guard against exposing themselves to complex products with high risks in order to satisfy their aggressive return targets. Certain pension funds will have constraints on investments due to their short-term liabilities; however, it is apparent now more than ever that sound long-term investment strategies will be required by U.S. pension funds to help meet their fiduciary obligations.[41]

The Characteristics of Private-Market Investing

Private-market investing is an umbrella term encapsulating a variety of illiquid investments that cannot be sold at short notice and therefore require a long-term investment horizon and patient capital. These types of investments, which provide the focus for this book, include infrastructure, renewable energy, agriculture, natural resources, real estate, venture capital, and private equity. The opaque nature of private-market assets and various information asymmetries has meant that a relational form of delegated investing has been adopted by institutional investors for accessing these assets, with a large reliance on intermediaries for the investment process. This is in contrast to direct investing or co-investing, where capital is deployed directly into the asset or company.

Private companies are not subjected to the information disclosure regulations that publicly listed companies must adhere to, giving investment managers the opportunity to gain access to and act on information not readily available in the public domain. Investments in private markets also often require managing the assets actively, playing a material role in growing the assets, and adding significant value over the investment period. Investment management firms have investment professionals dedicated to taking advantage of informational asymmetries in private markets and have the necessary skill set for sourcing, analyzing, executing, and managing long-term assets. For these reasons, many institutional investors without sufficient governance and resource capability have used the services of third-party investment managers and consultants for making investments into private markets.

Investors in private markets should thus expect higher returns compared with public markets because of the premium paid for illiquidity and other asset-specific risks. While the benefits from each asset class vary (as well as the data and benchmark used for comparisons), substantial empirical evidence suggests that private market investing can offer greater returns over investing in the public markets.[42] This is particularly true for private equity and real estate. While venture capital fund returns outperformed public equities in the 1990s, they have underperformed in the most recent decade.[43] Infrastructure is a relatively new private-market asset class, and so reliable returns data is quite limited. Early studies have shown that infrastructure has been mixed with a large amount of variation in the types of assets and subsequent returns achieved.[44]

The allocation of institutional investors to private markets has been increasing over time. Andonov (2014), based on the CEM database,[45] shows that institutional investors in developed economies have increased their allocation to alternative assets (which also includes hedge funds) from 8 percent in 1990 to more than 15 percent in 2011. He finds that larger institutional investors have increased their allocation in a higher proportion. Larger investors not only allocate a greater percentage of their assets to alternative investments but are more likely to invest simultaneously in multiple alternative asset classes. In addition to size, institutional investors that diversify their public equity investment internationally also invest a higher percentage of their total assets in multiple alternative asset classes at the same time. Institutional investors that use more active rather than passive management in public equity are investing relatively more in alternative asset classes, where passive investing is virtually impossible. The results suggest that institutional investors do not substitute active management in public equity with alternative investments but rather engage simultaneously in active investing in public and private markets. Most industry-based publications and surveys would indicate that institutional investors will be increasing their allocation to private-market asset classes over the next few years and beyond.[46] Understanding the most efficient access points for these investments will be ever more important.

The Challenges with Delegated Investing

Investing through external managers is the dominant investment approach for institutional investors accessing private markets. Sponsors of institutional investor organizations have been happy to let the fund's performance be dependent on the oversight of a long chain of principal agent relationships typically with consultants, fund of funds, and asset managers. Although this method of investing seemed to work for a while, more recently, the GFC exposed the incorporation of incentives at each link of the chain that distorted the original motives of the asset owners. Early studies suggested that many private-equity limited partnerships (LPs) do not outperform public-market benchmarks despite a private-equity boom occurring in the years leading up to the crisis.[47] While managers exhibited a certain amount of investment skill as depicted by their gross returns being greater than public-equity benchmarks, the lack of superior return for the LPs implied that "rents" were earned by asset managers. Whatever outperformance might have been achieved may not account for the higher risk (e.g., leverage) and illiquidity of the transactions.[48]

Agency problems in delegated asset management can occur because the asset owner and the fund manager may have different utilities or risk aversions, incentives, horizons, skills, information sets, or interests. In addition, the principal's ability to monitor the agent is limited, as it could be expensive or the asset owner may not understand the information being uncovered in the monitoring process. Principals lack the ability to judge whether the agent has talent or is doing a good job. Adverse selection and moral hazard originating from the insurance industry explain the agency problems in delegated institutional investment.[49]

The principal-agent issues associated with asset management have also been compared to the issue of "broken agency" apparent in the construction industry between the short-term contractors that bear short-term risk and the managers that bear the long-term risk and rewards of the project.[50] The misaligned objectives between the two parties can lead to suboptimal outcomes. In the case of institutional investor organizations, broken agency affects how assets are allocated. There may be a severe disconnect between the types of assets and risks that an investor may think they are being exposed to and the actual investments being made by their short-term-oriented asset managers. A way of realigning interests would be to identify asset managers that have the same long-term objectives as the asset owner. The challenge for investors is to determine how they can incorporate their long-term interests in the design and framing of short-term investment policies and strategies.

The biggest issue with regard to delegated investing is the significant costs associated with employing intermediaries to deploy capital. External investment costs include the management fees paid to investment consultants and external asset managers, performance fees, carried interest, and rebates, which are directly subtracted from the returns and are not incorporated into cost figures. External costs also include costs (compensation, benefits, travel, and education costs) for internal staff whose sole responsibility is to select and monitor external managers in alternative assets. On top of the fees, the costs of internal resourcing can be substantial to ensure that the appropriate sophistication is present to get access to the outperformance of top managers (as per the endowment model).[51]

From the CEM benchmarking database, it was deduced that the average private-equity annual cost was 3.41 percentage points, followed by hedge funds at 1.43 and real assets at 0.84.[52] These figures, however, also include investors who have used internal teams to access the asset classes. The typical "2-and-20" external private-equity fund compensation structure can result in a cumulative investment cost of 5 to 7 percentage points per year under a wide range of performance assumptions and after portfolio construction costs have been accounted for.[53] If investors are expecting a 5 percent illiquidity premium on these private-market assets, they may end up spending the entire premium on fees.

In some cases, asset management firms have misled investors about the fees that they are charging. Many LTIs present incomplete fee pictures in their annual reports; some funds focus only on base fees and bury performance fees in net return numbers, while others make no attempt to quantify the implicit fees associated with holding, moving, or trading assets (despite the fact that the implicit numbers, such as spreads and transaction costs, can be very high).

The attachment of early infrastructure funds to the investment banking industry illustrates the conflicts of interest arising for institutional investors. First, the fees charged by managers have been excessively high, resembling private-equity fees, despite private-equity returns being higher. This has typically involved a base management fee of 1 to 2 percent and performance fees of 10 to 20 percent, with an 8 to 12 percent hurdle rate.[54] Investors have also been concerned over the short time horizon of fund managers, with most funds offering closed-end models around 10 years with an investment holding period of 4 to 5 years. Investors, on the other hand, have been attracted to the asset class for the long duration of investments that can be held for 30 to 50 years. Also, certain organizations lack financial discipline and are conflicted in their motives. These factors have led some investors to find alternatives to the fund manager route, although most do not have the internal resources to be able to invest directly in infrastructure themselves or through co-investments. Whether they invest directly or indirectly, the development of strong relationships among investment partners is crucial for success.[55]

There are signs that the principal-agency issues in investment management are coming to light and are being addressed. The industry has seen a number of changes compared to the pre-crisis era. In August 2015, one of the largest institutional private-equity investors indicated that it will no longer invest in funds that do not disclose all of their fees.[56] The SEC has started to fine certain managers that were guilty of excessively and opaquely charging fees to their investors (although the amounts of the SEC fines have not been commensurate with the amounts of fees that the managers have been charging). Phalippou and colleagues (2015) have shown that half of the private-equity managers that historically charged the highest fees have not been able to raise a new fund since the financial crisis, and the managers that charged the least have all raised a new fund.

Direct Investing the Answer?

As a result of the issues raised previously, there is a growing trend among large institutional investors such as SWFs and large pension funds to reduce the agency problems in the investment management industry by in-sourcing more of their investment operations. Institutional investors believe that in-sourcing can provide benefits from a number of factors. First, sometimes third-party vehicles are not attractive, and *access* to a given asset can be more effectively achieved on a direct basis. When an investor's internal resources are developed, all aspects of the organization's capabilities can be improved as internal teams identify previously unknown gaps in the business. Perhaps the most common reason for in-sourcing is to maximize net-of-fee investment returns and minimize agency costs.[57]

Despite the benefits, replicating the external market for financial services within a single institutional investor organization raises significant issues related to scale and expertise. Only the very large investor organizations are capable of incorporating traditionally outsourced functions and invest in assets that provide a risk-adjusted return that meets the needs of their beneficiaries.

Size alone, however, does not guarantee success for in-sourcing. With increasing size and complexity come issues of organizational inertia. Without market rivalry and competition for such services, or a limited scope for interorganizational knowledge transfers and spillovers, there is a risk of organizational sclerosis. Coupled with the challenge of how to govern a range of functions, bringing more of the market within the organization is risky. Hence, there are robust organizational reasons why most beneficiary institutions continue to outsource the management of assets to service providers in major international financial centers. Other challenges associated with in-sourcing include attracting and retaining adequate human resources, achieving necessary scale of in-house capabilities to be able to build a diversified portfolio, and overcoming the loss of scale economies realized in their relationships with intermediaries.

In-sourcing requires investors to attract talent with specialist skills and operational expertise on investments but also in risk and compliance. This will require the design of competitive compensation packages. Investors also need to incorporate the technology to assess risk and performance across multi-asset portfolios. In-sourcing thus requires an overhaul of a fund's operating models and data infrastructures. The in-sourcing requirements can be challenging if the transition is not thought through comprehensively. The Korea Investment Corporation (KIC) is an example of an institutional investor that was unable to execute a direct investing strategy successfully. The direct deals that it had carried out in the early 2000s fared worse than its fund investments, and this was primarily due to a lack of knowledge and experience.[58] In the case of KIC, not enough attention had been paid to due diligence and risk management, and the organization had relied too heavily on the recommendations of investment advisors.

In order to be an effective in-house investor, good governance is crucial, as it is the primary mechanism to mobilize the resources of an institution. Direct investors need to streamline the investment decision-making process and be able to move at the pace of transactions. Investment committees that might comprise the board need to break from "calendar time" meeting schedules and be prepared to meet in real time. In general, the governance budget required for in-sourcing will depend on the stock of organizational resources, including the talent and skills of portfolio managers, the processes and protocols of decision making, and the information processing tools that support judgments.[59] In summary, it is the people, processes, protocols and systems that are essential for direct investing. The authors acknowledge that gaining these resources and organizational improvements is no easy task. Failure to take the right precautions and steps could lead to undesirable outcomes.[60]

The attributes required by organizations for in-sourcing can be ranked as fundamental (people, organizational, risk management), intermediate (culture, asset selection, mandates) and advanced (delegation and segregation, communication, networks).[61] It is the last advanced attribute of networks that this book in part proposes as a way to help investor organizations develop some of the other attributes for more efficient long-term investing. A report by the World Economic Forum on direct investing indicates that the progression toward direct investing might be gradual, in which asset owners, having decided to invest in an illiquid asset class such as infrastructure, may use external mandates initially, but gradually move into co-investing with fund managers before gaining enough experience and organizational sophistication that the asset owner is able to optimize their access to the asset class through direct investing.[62] In sum, while direct investing would be the most preferred method for institutional investors, it has significant challenges and risks. The collaborative model, which combines direct investing and delegated investing based on forming innovative partnerships, is proposed as a possible alternative to help achieve the long-term investment objectives of institutional investors.

A Framework for Reframing Finance

At the start of this chapter, we proclaimed that the financial crisis exposed a number of inefficiencies and opaque practices within global capital markets. Traditional academic thinking in finance and economics has also come under much scrutiny. Economic geographer and Nobel Prize winner Paul Krugman stated, "Economists fell back in love with the old, idealized vision of an economy in which rational individuals interact in perfect markets."[63] Prominent Berkeley economist Barry Eichengreen proclaimed that "the great credit crisis has cast into doubt much of what we knew about economics." He went on to say that while the twentieth century focused on "deductive economics," the twenty-first century will be all about "inductive economics" with research grounded in concrete observations of markets and their inhabitants.[64] As a result, economists have become more interested in explaining the social, political, and geographical dimensions of economic life. In an attempt to supplement their theoretical arguments with more intensive empirical research, economists have moved closer to a social perspective as well as to sociology.

In order to understand the evolving dynamics of institutional investor organizations, their agents, and their relationships with capital markets, we adopt an economic sociology and geography approach in this book. We draw upon many useful works within finance and economics, but the application of economic sociology and economic geography to study institutional investor investment decision making represents a novel way of approaching this evolving research area.

The field of modern economic sociology was manifested by Mark Granovetter's paper titled "Economic Action and Social Structure: The Problem of Embeddedness."[65] Granovetter's research grew out of the realization that the weakest point in economics analysis is the neglect of social structure. He therefore argued that sociologists should attempt to embed economic actions in social structure, conceived as ongoing interpersonal networks.[66] Economic sociology, as used in this book, draws on social network ideas, organization theory, and the sociology of contracts. Economic geography, which in part stems from economic sociology, helps conceptualize the geographic and political embeddedness of institutional investment. In particular, we build on the work of Gordon Clark, who in many ways pioneered the field of institutional investor governance within economic geography.

• • •

From Granovetter and Swedberg's *The Sociology of Economic Life*, we would like to highlight three basic principles of economic sociology:

1. Economic action is a form of social action. While economics adopts the rather unrealistic actor—*Homo economicus*—sociology takes real actors in their interactions as the point of departure. Economic actions typically are not only determined by self-interest. Trust, norms, and power influence economic actions and therefore invalidate the pure self-interest assumption. Related to this, no economic action takes place in an abstract space; there is always a broader social context, which affects the actions of the individual. Economic sociology emphasizes that an actor's search for approval, status, sociability, and power cannot be separated from economic action. The decision to work for an asset management firm over an asset owner is an example of this. In this way, economic sociology may be more broadly equipped to deal with different empirical issues. A further example arises when analyzing investment management contracts. The financial services industry has accumulated a lot of wealth and power over the last few decades, which has consolidated their bargaining status and at times led to opaque contractual arrangements. We argue that a sociological approach, which takes into account trust-based relational contracting norms and recognizes the characteristics and wider needs of both parties, is needed when formulating investment management contracts.

2. Economic action is socially situated, embedded in ongoing networks of personal relationships, rather than being carried out by "atomized actors." *Network* in this context means a regular set of contacts or social connections among individuals or organizations. Action by a network member is embedded, since it is carried out through interacting with other people. Networks are important in finance, and the existence of certain financial intermediaries is due to the way networks are structured in the investment management process. Institutional investors should systematically build an efficient and

effective network to help them gain access to attractive investment opportunities as well as to help with knowledge sharing and general organizational development.

3. Economic institutions are social constructions. Rather than considering institutions an objective, external reality, here we propose that they are typically the result of slow, social creation. Granovetter conceptualized the idea of path-dependent development to organizational and institutional forms. He argues that "economic institutions are constructed by the mobilization of resources through social networks, conducted against a background of constraints given by previous historical development of society, polity, market and technology."[67] Networks play a significant role especially at an early stage in the formation of an economic institution. It is crucially important to understand the historical development of institutional investor organizations in order to appreciate how these institutions might be able to invest. Certain pension funds have well-ingrained structures and processes with strict regulations constraining their ability to invest. Sovereign wealth funds, on the other hand, are newer organizations and may have a better ability to attract talent, make decisions quickly, and adopt innovative strategies for investment management. While a number of strategies are proposed in this book, we acknowledge that their implementation is organizationally and geographically dependent. Similarly, we also propose that some of the practices of asset managers, the same practices that have been carried out over the last two decades, need to change. Understanding the historical context helps to acknowledge the inertia and difficulty that may be encountered in promoting change.

• • •

This book takes the lens of institutional investors to understand how more long-term capital can be channeled efficiently into long-term private-market assets. We essentially draw on theoretical and empirical evidence to illustrate how the collaborative model of institutional investment is being shaped and defined. Specifically, the collaborative model of long-term investing proposed here draws on social network theory to understand how institutional investors can not only help develop their own internal expertise but form deep, trusting relationships with potential investment partners. The re-intermediation thesis uses the concept of embeddedness to define how more alignment can be achieved in the transaction between asset owners and asset managers. Case studies that are emblematic of the collaborative/partnership-based model of

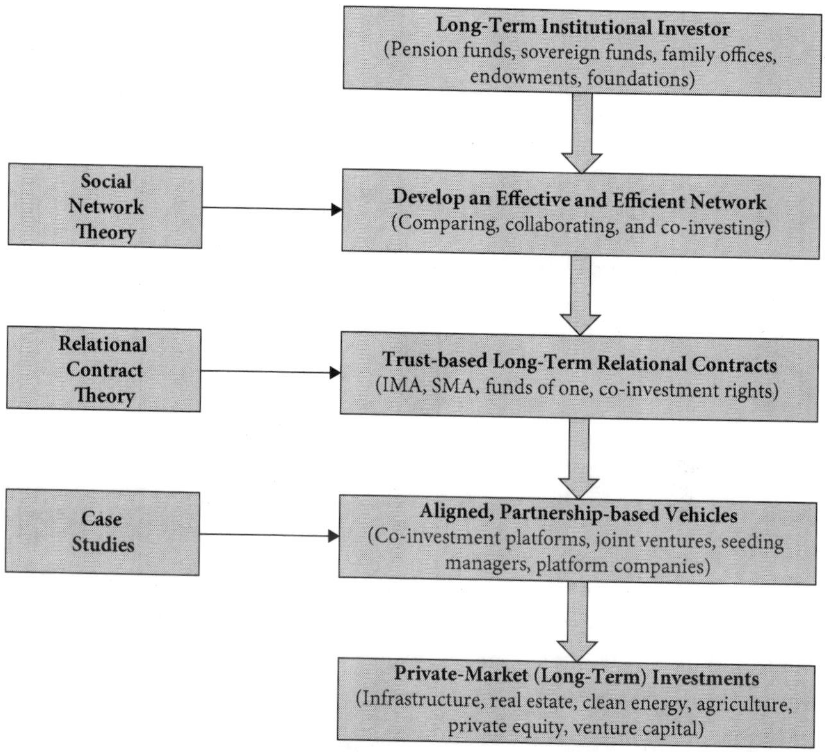

FIGURE 1.4 Rationale for the collaborative model of institutional investment

private-market institutional investment are illustrated to show how these initiatives are being developed, which are likely to influence how the industry will be shaped in the future. The rationale for the collaborative/partnerships-based model and structure of this book is outlined in Figure 1.4.

As mentioned, the motivation for the work in this book comes from the need to further understand the evolving dynamics of institutional investor organizations and determine how these investors can channel their capital into "real," long-term investments. The collaborative model combines elements of other methods of institutional investment but is distinct and new enough to warrant a detailed theoretical underpinning and a consolidation of the key characteristics. The motivation also comes from the need to understand how these trends might affect the role that different actors and agents will play in the institutional investment management process.

2 Building an Institutional Investor's Collaborative Network and Social Capital

IN MANY RESPECTS, it is the network of an intermediary, rather than its know-how or domain expertise, that provides the most value-add in the investment management process and, in turn, allows an investment bank, placement agent, or investment manager to charge high fees. Investor organizations that hope to minimize the fees paid, and thus maximize investment returns, must identify new, more-aligned collaborators and partners that can help bolster and replace the network access that traditional third parties are ultimately selling. In our view, a robust network can help an investor overcome their historical reliance on financial intermediaries for deploying capital. Developing a strong, effective network may help a long-term investor address some of the key gaps in their knowledge, human resources, or even risk management, thereby improving sophistication and facilitating more efficient investing.

Encouragingly, these claims—specifically that there are significant benefits for institutional investors in developing their social capital—are supported by a growing body of academic studies focused on social network theory. In fact, grounded in sociological research, social network theory informs us how a network can help long-term investors carry out their function more effectively. As Burt (1992) states: "Something about the structure of the player's network and the location of the player's contacts in the social structure of the arena provides a competitive advantage in getting higher rates of return on investment." As readers can guess, then, in the field of finance, investment performance has been tightly linked with the connectedness of the investing entity or individual.[1]

Historically, commercial and investment banks identified investment opportunities, valued transactions, negotiated deal terms, and financed growth. The key role of banks and asset managers was "to facilitate the formation of network ties between issuers and investors, to consolidate all information on the needs of the two groups, to arrange for issuer/investor ties; and to constitute the ties by consummating the transaction."[2] For a financial intermediary to be effective in soliciting business and in structuring transactions appropriately, it needed to constantly obtain information on issuers and investors. As one venture capital firm noted during our research: "In pursuing any given deal, ex ante, our biggest value is in our network."

Thus, by forming a strong network of peer investors and other organizations, LTIs can share local knowledge and asymmetric information as well as pool skill sets, deal pipelines, and networks with better alignment of interests than available with outsourced options. Since the 1970s, social network research in the organizational and interorganizational contexts has provided insight into the potential value for LTIs in proactively pursuing "social capital."[3] At the most general and basic level, *social capital* refers to the value attached to relationships. Studies on social capital have related an actor's ties to a wide range of outcomes such as mobility, individual performance, entrepreneurship, power, and individual creativity.

Social Capital Theory—General Features[4]

LTIs generally possess three main types of capital—financial, human, and social—to fulfill their roles and objectives in the finance industry and the larger capitalist ecosystem. Different from financial and human capital, which are solely owned by an organization or individual, social capital is loosely defined as the value of relationships with other social actors.[5] Thus, the parties to a relationship jointly own social capital. In other words, no one organization or individual has exclusive ownership rights to social capital. Furthermore, relationships with clients, colleagues, and friends can lead to opportunities where financial and human capital can be transformed into profit.[6]

The three core dimensions for the concept of social capital—structural, relational, and cognitive[7]—constitute three different sources of value associated with relationships. Specifically, the structural dimension of social capital is related to the value that can be achieved from one's position within the structure of a network, the relational dimension of social capital refers to the value associated with access to a variety of resources through network ties, and the cognitive dimension of social capital is often perceived as the value associated with shared representations, interpretations, and systems of meaning among network actors.

Although these dimensions are highly interconnected, historically they have been studied under different theoretical lenses. On the one hand, the structural and relational dimensions correspond to two theoretical frameworks of network research in the social sciences, that is, new economic sociology (or social network analysis) and social exchange theory (or exchange networks), respectively; on the other hand, the cognitive dimension has mainly received attention in the domains of strategy and social psychology.

To better understand how social capital theory can help inform the design of an efficient and effective collaborative investment network, we use a table (see Table 2.1) to briefly summarize the relevant literature along the three dimensions of social capital, with a focus on the implications for institutional investment.

Table 2.1 illustrates how the core theoretical concepts within the field of social capital can help inform and validate a collaborative networking strategy for LTIs. The intent is to provide an overview of the relevant theory to help understand the rationale for the collaborative model of institutional investment.

Investors have been increasing their allocations to private-market asset classes in order to diversify their portfolios and maximize their return, which has meant forming a wide array of relationships with various other entities, including consultants, advisors, and managers. The complex arena of private-market investing can be likened to a large web of interconnected investors who start at one end and weave their way through to the other end to get to the fruits or sources of return on their capital. Social capital theory thus helps assess how investors are positioned in the competitive web of institutional investment and informs us how the web can be rewoven to ensure that investors take a more efficient path to reach the ripest fruits.

Social capital theory also helps explain how financial intermediaries have taken advantage of the information asymmetries apparent in the private-market investment space to extract value for their own benefit. Specifically, structural holes between nonredundant contacts in a network explain the

TABLE 2.1 Three dimensions of social capital research

Dimension	*Concepts*	*Arguments*	*Implications*
Structural	Structural Hole (Burt 1992): The space between two actors when they are connected to the same other actor (i.e., the broker) but not connected to each other. Weak Tie (Granovetter 1973): The relationship that connects two actors who share little redundant information. Both structural holes and weak ties explain brokers' social capital, which include information and control benefits.	Brokers gain information benefits via three mechanisms: (1) *Access* refers to receiving valuable pieces of information and knowing who can use it. (2) *Timing* refers to receiving information before others. (3) *Referral* refers to the broker's name being mentioned at the right time and place to provide opportunities for the broker itself. Brokers also gain control benefits because with these information benefits, they can negotiate relationships with others.	The finance industry is filled with various types of brokers, namely, investment banks, investment consultants, placement agents, advisors, funds of funds, and investment management firms. Institutional investors, who are interested in long-term private market opportunities, can build a collaborative network to reduce their reliance on the preceding types of brokers, so that their investment capability and performance can be significantly improved.
Relational	Resource (Foa and Foa 1980): The political, information, goods/service, and financial assets that motivate exchange activities between network actors. Power (Weber 1978): The probability that one actor within a relationship will be in a position to carry out its own will despite resistance.	Power-Dependence Theory (Emerson 1962, 1972a, 1972b) and Resource Dependence Theory (Pfeffer 1972a, 1972b, 1972c, Pfeffer and Salancik 2003). The power of Actor A over Actor B equals B's dependence on the resources controlled by A.	The power of brokers in the finance industry comes from their control of the informational resources, but other types of resources are also critical for the performance of institutional investors and thus should be included in the consideration of power. An ego investor should first engage powerful investors to improve the effectiveness of its collaborative network.
Cognitive	Trust (Rotter 1967): A generalized expectancy held by an actor that the word of another actor can be relied on. Closure (Coleman 1988, 1990): The extent to which actors are connected to each other in a network.	Closure is often measured as density, which is the proportion of possible relationships that are present in the network. High closure promotes the communication between network actors and further brings the benefits of information richness and quality as well as group solidarity and trust.	For institutional investors and their brokers, one of the key issues from the recent financial crisis is the lack of trust in their relationships. Institutional investors need to maximize the efficiency of possible connections within a collaborative network to increase knowledge sharing and trust, which could improve performance.

presence of brokers (financial intermediaries). At the same time, social capital theory also highlights how the formation of strong bonds between LTIs based on trust can be used to bridge structural holes in their network in order to access vital resources such as attractive investment opportunities and achieve high rates of return.

The concept of weak ties informs us that more valuable information may be extracted from relationships with those outside our immediate social circles, and having primary contacts that introduce you to other social circles or clusters where nonredundant contacts are prevalent can provide more fruitful leads. But it is also important to maintain the strong ties of an investor to ensure that existing information benefits continue to accrue to the organization.

Private-market investing is complex, so developing a network among investor peers is important, not just for forming relationships with partners that can bring investment opportunities. Forming a network will also facilitate an investor's ability to fill the in-sourcing gaps in areas such as talent recruitment and organizational design and also to help others to fill their gaps. This is all part of an effort to help build a network of mutually beneficial, cooperative relationships over the long term. However, interpersonal relationships and issues of reciprocity will need to be addressed.

Social Network Theory—Finance/Investment Applications

We draw on social network theory to help understand how LTIs can better align their interests. A number of aspects have been studied under the umbrella of social network theory to better understand financial services. Network theories provide an alternative method for looking at finance and investment, especially where traditional theories and approaches may be limited. Certain assumptions in neoclassical finance, such as the efficient markets hypothesis, that actors behave rationally, and that actors maximize their own utility, do not hold in many real-world situations.

For example, with private-market investing, information on potential investment opportunities is not freely available, and since it is private and potentially valuable information, it may not be transmitted deliberately. Similarly, while market participants are utility maximizers, their utility function may incorporate nonmonetary, social dynamics such as the reciprocation of deal flow.[8] We highlight here some of the key studies that have used social network theory to analyze certain aspects of finance and investment management.

Network theories used to help understand financial systems have focused in part on addressing the issue of systemic risk, by determining how resilient financial networks are to contagion and how financial institutions (e.g., retail and commercial banks) form connections when exposed to propagating crises.[9] Network theory has even been used to explain freezes in the interbank market. In this context, the nodes of the network represent financial systems while the links are created through mutual exposures between banks, acquired on the interbank market holding similar exposures or by sharing the same mass of depositors.[10] The work also highlights that financial institutions can gain significant payoff advantages from bridging otherwise disconnected parts of the financial network. Hence, certain network structures may provide additional benefits for financial institutions that exploit their position as intermediaries between other institutions. Network structure can also play a role in how effective mutual monitoring is for the enforcement of risk-sharing agreements, as in microfinance.

Given the insights highlighted here, a growing literature is focused on the role social networks play in investment decisions and corporate governance. Some work has been done on public security markets: Cohen and colleagues (2007) use social networks to identify information transfers in security markets. They find that portfolio managers place larger bets on firms they are connected to through their network (such as former colleagues who went to the same college) and perform significantly better on these holdings relative to their nonconnected holdings.

Morrison and Wilhelm (2007) argue that investment banks exist primarily because they create networks between investors and investment opportunities. In the case of an initial public offering (IPO), investment banks acquire information about the demand for an issue from large investors such as pension funds and insurance companies to enable them to set a fair price. They also need to have a liquidity network to provide the funds to purchase the securities. On top of this, investment banks need to scour their network for investment opportunities or possible future deals. Morrison and Wilhelm note that, particularly when dealing with institutional investors, trust and reputation are crucial in these networks.

A number of studies have looked at the venture capital (VC) industry and in particular at VC firms that are connected through a network of syndicated portfolio investments.[11] VC firms tend to syndicate their investments with other VC firms, rather than investing alone.[12] While there are significant differences and dynamics between venture capital firms and asset owner LTIs, a number of lessons can be learned about the power of social capital and networks from the studies of networks of VC firms.

Hochberg and colleagues (2007), using graph theory to analyze a large sample of U.S. biotech-focused VC networks, find that better-networked VC firms can achieve better fund performance, as measured by the proportion of investments that are successfully exited through an IPO or a sale to another company. While their position in the VC network may be important for getting access to deal flow, the authors find that well-networked VC firms appear to perform better because they provide better value-added services to their portfolio companies.

The syndication of VC firms enhances their ability to source high-quality deal flow and support investments. For deal flow, VC firms invite others to co-invest in their promising deals in the expectation of future reciprocity. By working together, VC firms can collate correlated signals and therefore select better investments where there may be considerable uncertainty about potential investments.[13] Some VC firms may have sector- or geographic-specific expertise, and syndication helps share knowledge, allowing VC firms to diversify their portfolios.

With regard to portfolio investments, syndication networks facilitate the sharing of information, contacts, and resources among VC firms and could help, for example, with increasing the reach of launch customers or expanding strategic alliance partners for their portfolio companies. Strong relationships with other VC firms can also improve the chances of securing follow-on VC funding for portfolio companies and get access to other VC networks of head hunters, patent lawyers, and investment bankers to help their companies succeed.[14]

Bygrave (1988) argues that the primary reason for co-investing in venture capital is a sharing of knowledge rather than spreading of financial risk. When there is more uncertainty, the amount of co-investing increases, although the average amount invested per portfolio company is less. VC firms gather valuable strategic information about future innovations and technological trends from their emergent companies. This type of information, on top of the shared business plans, budgets, financial statements, and annual meetings, can be very valuable and accessed when partnering with other VC firms. The exchange of information is an important way of finding and evaluating investment opportunities. There are higher chances of success and firms are more likely to invest in a proposal that was referred to them than opportunities that come from unknown sources. A major source of referrals is other VC firms that want to syndicate an investment. The greater the number of co-investments, the stronger the ties and the greater the breadth of communication a firm can have.

While the structure and setup of LTIs differs from the structure of VC firms, numerous lessons can be applied to LTIs from the co-investing methods employed by venture capital firms. By engaging with other peer investors, LTIs not only may get access to private assets in a more aligned fashion but will also be working toward achieving other, wider long-term goals, in much the same way that VC firms have benefited from their syndication networks in unpredictable ways.

The literature review in this section provides useful insights for assessing how asset owners can invest in real assets more efficiently. However, there does not seem to be any work carried out on how LTIs (the actual owners of the capital) can use networks to help them cooperate, collaborate, or co-invest and subsequently develop organizational capacity and more efficiently deploy their capital in private-market asset classes.

Designing an Efficient and Effective Network: A Framework for Investors

Building on the theoretical and academic argument for a networking strategy, we provide guidance for how investors might systematically approach such a strategy. For this purpose (and to keep things simple), we define a generic collaborative investment network as an interorganizational network connecting like-minded peer investors to exchange valued resources and obtain better investment performance and enhanced investment capability. Within such a network, a wide range of explicit or implicit resources may be exchanged between institutional investors—for example, investment opportunities, co-investment capital, investment knowledge, and labor (temporary staff reassignments).

Our research over the past few years has found that LTIs seek to develop their network for three reasons: First, at the most basic level, investors look to cooperate or compare with other investors to help them maintain best practices within their own organization. Cooperation is the simplest way in which senior managers of a financial institution can extend their knowledge and understanding of strategic options to other institutions. Second, investors look to collaborate with peer investors on a bilateral or multilateral level, such as through staff exchanges and participating in research clubs and roundtables. Collaboration involves commitment to a project or projects in terms of both the specification of shared objectives and the means of realizing those objectives, and thus is likely to require a stronger legal framework than is the case with cooperation. Third, (and ultimately) investors look to develop their network to form efficient co-investment vehicles with trusted partners. Co-investment is the highest level of collaboration, and thus requires platforms and vehicles to align the interests, objectives, and responsibilities of investors. These three objectives—cooperation, collaboration, and co-investment—encapsulate the key tools of the collaborative model of institutional investment.

The key differences among these three objectives—cooperation, collaboration, and co-investment—are the types of resources and the levels of trust involved in the corresponding network relationships or exchange activities. For instance, information (intellectual capital), staff (human capital), and money (financial capital) are examples of resources exchanged through cooperation, collaboration, and co-investment among LTIs. Generally speaking, a higher level of trust is required when the relationships progress from cooperation to collaboration and then on to co-investment. As a result, we can treat cooperation, collaboration, and co-investment as three different stages in an evolving set of networking activities. As this implies, a coherent strategy may be required to coordinate all three types of activities, as cooperation may precede collaboration, which may precede co-investment. Note that for most institutional investors, those that operate entirely outsourced operations, these activities represent paradigm shifts in organizational strategy.

The network of peer investors is not only useful in helping them source investment opportunities but also critical to develop their organizational advantage (the ability to create and share knowledge)[15] and to transcend their home bias (the hegemony of local practice),[16] through pooling a variety of resources of different investors.

A collaborative investor network consisting of like-minded institutional investors (network actors) and a wide range of exchange activities (network relationships) between these investors can be proactively designed and optimized either for the benefit of a single network actor, whom we refer to as the ego, or for all the network actors as a whole. From a design or analysis perspective, these two focal points correspond to the egocentric or whole-network levels of analysis, respectively. In other words, the level of network analysis is derived either from the perception of one particular investor looking out or from a group of investors as a whole, such as those in a membership roundtable or research club. At the egocentric level, researchers typically focus on "the kind of effects that the ego's network has on its behavior and performance,"[17] whereas at the whole-network level, researchers focus on "the characteristics and behavior of the entire interorganizational network."[18]

Here, we look at the network design considerations from the perspective of an "ego investor,"[19] that is, the investor who sits in the center of a collaborative investment network, initiates network-building efforts, and actively seeks to use the network as a means to obtain better investment performance and enhanced investment capability.

While such a network may be most applicable for very large investors that can co-invest directly, we are also interested in institutional investors who are contemplating the current trend of direct investing but face the challenges of in-sourcing investment management functions. The types of ego investors applicable here would likely consist of large sovereign wealth funds (SWFs) (those with assets under management [AUM] of more than $5 billion), pension funds, insurance funds, endowments and foundations, and family offices, but not necessarily restricted just to these investors only.[20]

What Is an Efficient and Effective Network?

Our objective is to help investors design an efficient and effective network to ultimately help them obtain better investment performance and enhanced investment capability. We thus define *effectiveness* as the degree to which a network is successful in engaging the most important investors, that is, those that control valued resources and occupy critical positions in the network. This may include the investors that have access to the most sought-after deal flow, have developed more sophisticated thinking in areas such as environmental, social, and governance (ESG) factors or have deep experience investing in a particular area such as emerging economy infrastructure. We define *efficiency* as the degree to which a network can maximize the total value returned to the ego investor by allocating its own output resources. Output resources are the resources of the ego investor that are in most demand by other investors (opportunities, capital, knowledge, staff); that is, an ego investor's network is efficient if it is in contact with peer investors that value its own particular opportunities, knowledge, or staff.

These two definitions of effectiveness and efficiency provide two concrete, interrelated, and measurable objectives for the design of a collaborative investment network. They also enable network statistics to be constructed as a quantitative measure of the external and internal strengths of an ego investor. To put it differently, external strength (outside the organizational boundary of an ego investor) requires the ego investor to select the most important peer investors for collaboration, while internal strength (inside the organizational boundary of an ego investor) requires the ego investor to identify the most important output resources for the purpose of engaging selected peer investors.

From these two objectives, we can then derive three logical steps for the ego investor to build its collaborative investment network:

1. Selecting peer investors for collaboration
2. Constructing exchange activities with selected peer investors
3. Allocating output resources to develop the constructed exchange activities

The first two steps can be used to measure the external strength of an ego investor in terms of selecting the most important peer investors, and thus they can help the ego investor achieve network effectiveness. The third step is used to measure the internal strength of an ego investor by identifying the most important output resources for the purpose of engaging selected peer investors, and thus it can help the ego investor achieve network efficiency. Having defined effectiveness and efficiency and the related objectives, we will now discuss the factors that the ego investor needs to consider when carrying out these three steps.

Network Design Considerations

Power is a central consideration when it comes to the design of networks and particularly important in the finance industry. The concept of power is widely researched among management and social scientists, and numerous studies show that a network actor's power is determined by two factors: (1) the resources controlled by the network actor and (2) that actor's position in the network.[21] More specifically, if an actor controls critical resources needed by other actors and occupies a central position in the network, that actor will be interpreted as more powerful than others.

Through building network relationships with more powerful investors, it is reasonable to assume the ego investor will be able to access critical resources (e.g., investment opportunities) and meanwhile take advantage of the central positions (i.e., structural holes) of those investors. To put it differently, the resources and the position of a more powerful investor have the potential to create more value for the ego investor along the relational and structural dimensions of social capital, respectively.

From a psychological perspective, however, the power imbalance[22] between an ego investor and a selected peer investor could make it difficult for the ego investor to directly engage with the peer investor in the form of a bilateral exchange. For example, a large SWF may be reluctant to directly engage with a less-significant pension fund when that pension fund tries to build its collaborative investment network. Under such a circumstance, we suggest the use of multilateral exchanges to indirectly engage the selected peer investor; that is, engaging with less-powerful investors initially may enable access to the more powerful investors. Bilateral and multilateral exchanges represent two basic patterns of exchange activities in human society:[23] (1) in bilateral or restricted exchange, the two-party reciprocal relationships may be shown graphically as A ↔ B, and (2) in multilateral or generalized exchange, the univocal reciprocal relationships among at least three parties may be shown graphically as A → B → C → D → A. If C is a powerful investor, A may get access to C via B.

Compared to restricted exchanges, the importance of generalized exchanges has not yet been fully appreciated by researchers and practitioners, but the multilateral form of exchange activities opens the door to a wide range of strategies for an ego investor to access desired resources in an indirect way and thus reduce its dependence on powerful peer investors. Moreover, generalized exchanges are mainly bounded by trust and social norms and therefore make it possible for many types of resources, such as the information, goods/services, and financial resources discussed earlier, to be exchanged through network relationships. Restricted exchanges, however, are mainly bounded by clearly stated economic contracts and therefore may limit the types of exchangeable resources within goods/services and financial resources.

That being said, we recognize the potential moral hazard (inappropriate usage of asymmetric information), free-riding (taking without giving), and other social dilemmas associated with generalized exchanges, as this pattern of exchange activity does not require immediate reciprocity.[24] There are interesting insights from economics and behavioral sciences, such as network game theory[25] and stag hunter games,[26] which can help an ego investor avoid or minimize potential social dilemmas. For example, interactions between the ego investor and other investors to build a collaborative investment network can be modeled as cooperative network games. For these types of games, the stag hunt[27] provides a useful model to understand how the social contract between institutional investors looking for mutual benefits can play out; that is, a cooperation strategy can result in equilibrium for the whole network, but in the meantime, it carries risk (e.g., moral hazard and free-riding) and thus requires the development and maintenance of trust among all the participating investors. The evolution of the social contract between institutional investors can be seen as the process of moving from a riskless equilibrium of "hunting hare" to a risky but rewarding equilibrium of "hunting stag" (where a stag is a lot more valuable than a hare). Investors need to consider a number of factors when developing the implied social contract.

Additionally, to implement generalized exchanges as effective strategies in practice, an ego investor can also apply signaling mechanisms to better infer the quality of other investors and, in the meantime, better indicate its own quality, for the purpose of constructing sustainable and long-lasting network relationships.[28] For example, if the ego investor wants to choose a newly created fund as a partner for a collaborative investment, the quality (e.g., the capability, performance, and credibility of investment) of the potential partner can often be inferred from the organization's or individual's relationships with other high-status institutional investors. If an ego investor wants to signal its own good quality for the purpose of expanding its collaborative investment network, forming an alliance with a large well-reputed or well-established institutional investor can often be taken as an effective means.

These two principles—selecting powerful peer investors for collaboration and constructing generalized exchanges with peer investors who are difficult to engage directly—provide practical guidelines for an ego investor to complete the first two steps of designing a collaborative investment network. For the third step of network design, we suggest that an ego investor focus its efforts on the output resources that can maximize the value returned through all the possible exchange activities with peer investors.

In order to do so, an ego investor must acquire a deep understanding of the specific needs of each peer investor as well as of the preference levels of that investor for different resources. A simple example of this is as follows: a very large SWF in Asia may put a higher priority on investment opportunities (especially in other geographical locations) than on financial capital, which it already has a lot of. In the real world, information about the needs of peer investors and their preferences can be much more complicated. Relationships between investors can be a lot more involved than just the exchange of opportunities, capital, knowledge, or staff. An ego investor should keep in mind that obtaining granular information can be difficult (because of confidentiality considerations) and may be easily subject to change (because of the dynamic environment).

However, such an understanding sheds light on the motivations for institutional investors to enter into a variety of exchange activities and choose high-leverage output resources to build network relationships. The value of this understanding will depend on how rich the information is that an ego investor can collect from its peer investors, where the trust between these investors is a key issue. Through this exercise, the ego investor can develop meaningful organizational capability, which allows different teams within that investor to surface implicit assumptions about peer investors and share important knowledge that is otherwise difficult to express or communicate. Such an exercise helps the ego investor capture the value created along the cognitive dimension of social capital.

The preceding guidelines, summarized in Figure 2.1, formulate a comprehensive framework to help an ego investor design its collaborative investment network for the development of social capital. This framework provides a simple way for an investor to start implementing a collaboration strategy. As relationships become more complex and dynamic, a software tool would likely be needed to manage the network. A software tool would be important for aggregating the social capital of individuals in the organization as a whole in order to capture and manage this information even if those individuals left the firm. The usefulness of such a tool, however, will depend on the richness of data acquired and inputted to the model.

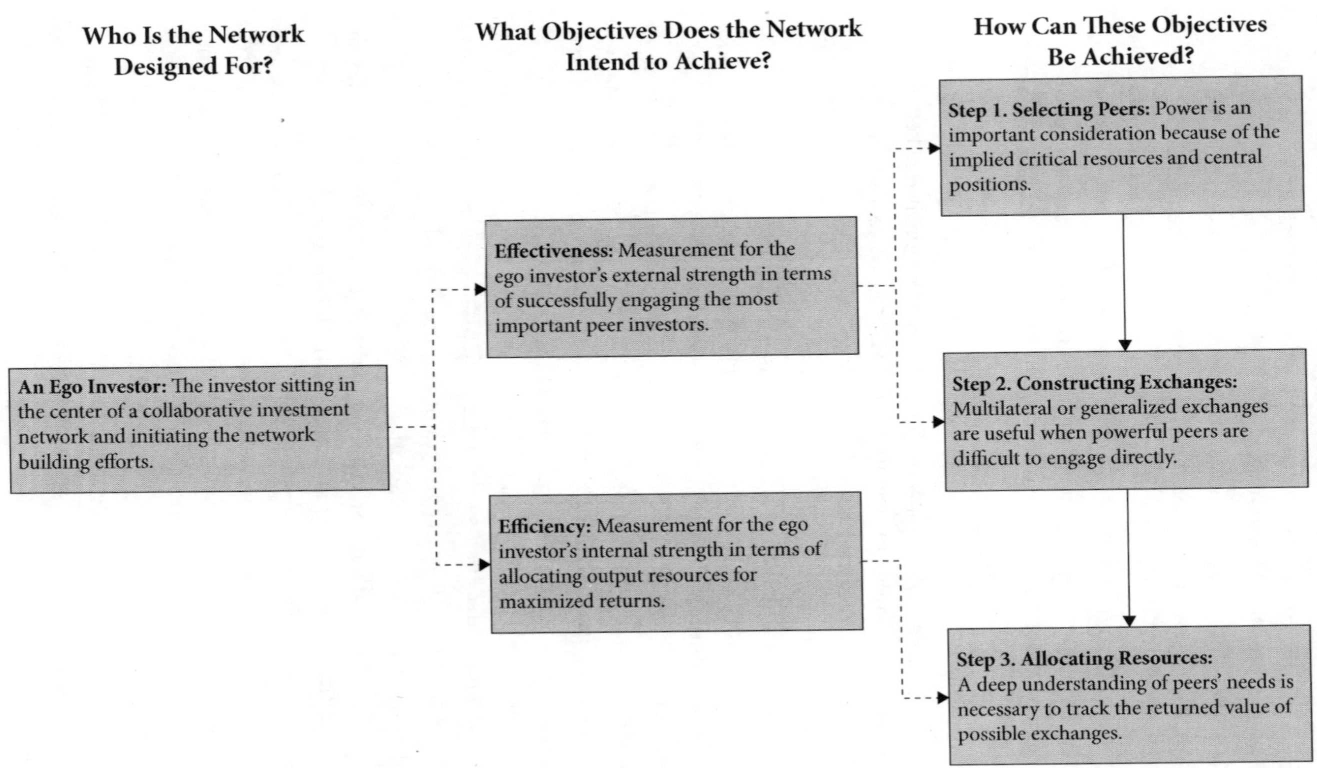

FIGURE 2.1 Guidelines for the design of a collaborative investment network

Horizontal Collaboration Versus Vertical Capital Deployment

The preceding network design guidelines focus on a horizontal form of collaboration. More specifically, they assess how institutional investors can build trusted relationships with peer investors to mutually help them achieve their long-term investment objectives through shared knowledge and opportunities. We assume that through the horizontal networking process, LTIs will be able to get vertical access to investment opportunities in a more aligned fashion. Access to opportunities may occur through the peer networking exercise (as discussed earlier); however, this may also require investors to develop relationships with other types of organizations and individuals. The sourcing of opportunities is a large part of the value that asset management firms bring to the investment management process. The sources of opportunities would depend in large part on the type of assets that the investors are looking to invest in.

For example, as outlined previously, a lot of the deal flow for VC investors comes from the network that they have created with other VC firms that they have previously syndicated with, as well as special relationships with universities and incubators. Private-equity, real estate, agriculture, and timber asset managers have dedicated teams scouring the market for opportunities, through either proprietary relationships with investment banks or other actors in specific sectors or regions. A key issue for asset owners to note is that a presence is required in these markets to take advantage of the networking dynamics associated with these sources of deal flow. This may mean having offices set up in the regions where the opportunities are based or having key personnel as trusted points of contact acting on behalf of the organization in these markets.[29] This has started to happen, for example, with certain asset owners setting up offices in San Francisco in order to get exposure to VC technology investing. Other investors have started to employ personnel from within certain specialist industries (forestry workers for timber, farm owners for agriculture) to look after their sector portfolios, bringing with them crucial contacts for deal flow and other aspects of investing in these areas. At the very least, investment professionals at asset owner organizations should not only be covering the key asset managers in certain asset classes but should also be identifying where the underlying assets are coming from. These are crucial steps for asset owners to build their networked economies in order to reduce their reliance on the agglomeration economies that have been established by asset management firms.

Infrastructure assets or urban development projects are quite different from other asset classes in that the investment opportunities stem directly from local, state, or central government agencies. The networking exercise in this case would require institutional investors to develop relationships with these government actors. At the heart of the relationship between asset owner investors and governments is the long-term value-add that such a relationship can produce over and above the short-term opportunistic nature of other asset manager investors. Infrastructure assets, which essentially are public goods, are long-term in nature. Governments need to form partnerships with alternative sources of finance in order to meet their infrastructure investment needs. The infrastructure public procurement process has been plagued with short-term investors bidding large premiums for assets, using financial leverage to extract value from the assets and then selling them off in order to return money to their investors and themselves under the limited partnership fund structure. This model of private infrastructure investing was exposed after the 2008–2009 financial crisis, with a number of investors being burned badly.

Alternatively, once large sums of long-term institutional investor capital have been pooled together in efficient investor-driven vehicles, governments should recognize the value of partnering with these long-term players in order to develop partnerships that can help service some of their infrastructure financing issues. Such partnerships have started to occur with governments understanding the value that can accrue back to the state through the financing of large infrastructure projects by pension funds and SWFs.[30] In this way, horizontal networking among peer investors should be complemented with clear strategies for how capital can reach the ground in real investment opportunities and the associated necessary relationships that need to be formed. This discussion emphasizes that developing social capital is both geographically and politically embedded.

Facilitating Collaborations Among Long-Term Investors

A number of other initiatives can help facilitate and realize a collaboration strategy for an investor in practice. These include roundtables and research clubs at the simpler end of the spectrum compared to more complex options, such as seeding related ventures, informal and formal partnerships, investment clubs, and shared-equity vehicles.

Roundtables/research clubs help investors improve their ability to cooperate and develop an efficient and effective network. The role of roundtables and research clubs for facilitating a network for investors is highlighted in Figure 2.2 (moving from step 1 to step 3) and is discussed in this chapter along with an analysis of some of the main examples currently active for LTIs. In Chapter 4, we look in more detail at the formal collaborative vehicles that have been established for LTIs, in particular co-investment platforms (step 3 to step 4).

Membership Roundtables/Research Clubs for Building an Investor's Network

The simplest category of initiatives that facilitate collaboration and cooperation among LTIs are research clubs and international roundtables that are set up to bring investors together to discuss various issues and concerns. These initiatives are usually set up by third parties to help facilitate cooperative endeavors being undertaken by LTIs by organizing meetings, roundtables, and releasing research papers. Some events mix together asset owners and managers, whereas others exclude asset managers to reduce marketing activity and instead help build aligned coalitions or alliances among the LTIs.

In weighing whether a senior manager of an investor organization should attend a roundtable or meeting, consideration would be given to who the other attendees may be, what topics will be presented, and what opportunity may exist to develop relationships away from the main program. The roundtables provide information with which to challenge internal teams and importantly help senior managers to distinguish that which is widely accepted and conventional from that which is unconventional and innovative. Ultimately, investor roundtables provide an opportunity to network and be exposed to personnel and organizations that would otherwise be hard to access. In this way, attending roundtables is a key stepping-stone for LTIs to reap the benefits of collaboration and develop an effective network.

Research clubs are an extension of the roundtables offered to investors, which may be a more "intimate" offering for LTIs. Indeed, research clubs can provide a more closed, focused setting for participants, enabling closer

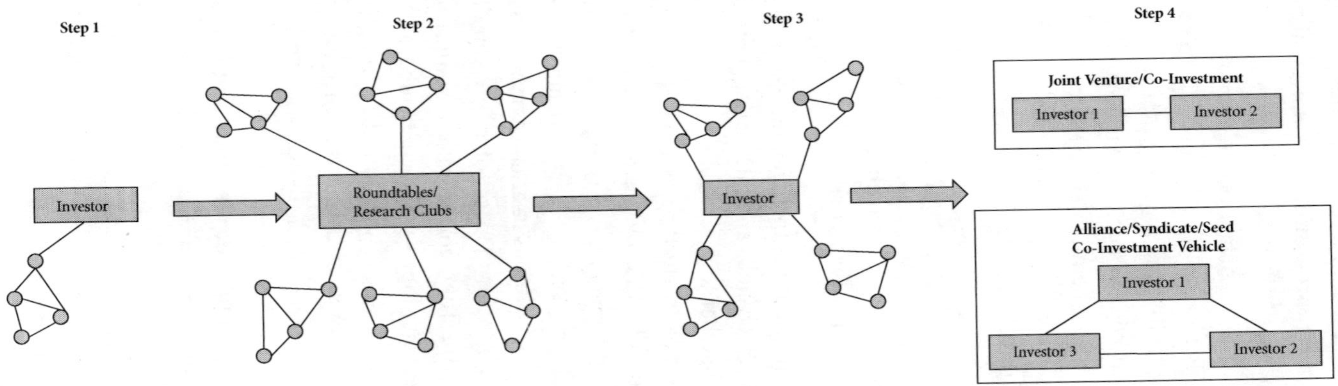

FIGURE 2.2 Progressive steps for developing an investor's network and collaborating

relationships to be formed but also ensuring that participants can learn from each other. New entrants may have the opportunity to invite other institutions with resources, skills, and capabilities that are consistent but also diversified with existing participants. An important consideration is to ensure that the size of the club remains manageable and the benefits keep accruing to members. The club's longevity will also depend on the extent to which fresh ideas offered to participants are maintained.

With growing awareness of the importance of long-term investing, a number of initiatives have been developed to help facilitate the most efficient deployment of capital by LTIs.

Institutional Investors Roundtable

The Institutional Investors Roundtable (IIR) was initially created in 2009 by the Quebec City Conference (QCC), a not-for-profit organization supported by the governments of Canada and Quebec and by private sponsors. The mission of QCC is to support private investment activities producing societal benefit by establishing forums of aligned stakeholders aimed at solving specific market dislocations. In October 2011, the IIR was spun out of the QCC to provide it with its own governance, while remaining contractually committed to support QCC's larger mission to produce societal benefit. Its members are: Abu Dhabi Investment Authority (ADIA), ATP (Denmark), British Columbia Investment Management Corporation (bcIMC), Caisse de dépôt et placement du Québec, Caisse des dépôts et consignations (France), Canada Pension Plan Investment Board (CPPIB), China Investment Corporation, GIC Special Investments Pte Ltd (Singapore), Ontario Teachers' Pension Plan, PGGM (Netherlands), Queensland Investment Corporation (QIC, Australia), Russian Direct Investment Fund (RDIF), Temasek International Pte Ltd (Singapore), TIAA (U.S.) and Founding CEO Christian Racicot.

The IIR, in its current form, is a not-for-profit platform exclusively for strategic leaders of global LTIs to explore ways to improve collaboration among them and to consider tangible and innovative ways to co-invest and foster relationships of trust, which are key to their long-term cooperation.

The IIR holds two formal meetings annually. The spring meeting is hosted by IIR participants on a rotating basis, and the fall meeting is normally held in Quebec City. In principle, the IIR is open to all interested and like-minded investors who accept the rules of engagement adopted by the board of directors; however, IIR is not open to investors significantly engaged in managing assets for third parties.

Examples of collaboration opportunities that have been presented or spun out as a result of the IIR meetings include a $10 billion co-investment vehicle to attract large-scale investments in Russia (RDIF), presentation of a long-term co-investment vehicle in agriculture (TIAA-CREF), a large-scale co-investment opportunity to acquire strategic national assets (CDC France), and a co-investment opportunity in a portfolio of early-stage fast-growing and potentially disruptive technology companies (Innovation Alliance).

International Forum of Sovereign Wealth Funds

The International Forum of Sovereign Wealth Funds (IFSWF) was borne out of the International Working Group of Sovereign Wealth Funds following their meeting in Kuwait City on April 5–6, 2009. The IFSWF was inaugurated as a nonprofit organization for sovereign wealth funds to meet and discuss issues of interest to the group and facilitate an understanding of the Santiago Principles.[31]

The IFSWF consists of twenty-seven members who meet once a year at one of the member institution countries. Each annual gathering consists of two to three days of meetings, some of which are closed for members while others more widely open in a standard presentation/discussion format. Membership to the IFSWF is by application with approval made by the board. The secretariat for the IFSWF was originally attached to the International Monetary Fund (IMF) but now operates independently with headquarters in London.

The IFSWF was set up to operate in an inclusive manner and facilitate communication among SWFs, representatives of other multilateral organizations, and the private sector. The first directive for IFSWF members is to understand the experiences of applying the Santiago Principles to date. Second, the IFSWF seeks to compare and contrast member investment and risk management practices. Third, it tries to facilitate a more favorable international investment environment and develop recipient country relationships.

Long-Term Investors Club

The Long-Term Investors Club (LTIC) was founded in 2009 with the aim of "bringing together major worldwide institutions and to encourage them to affirm their identity as long-term investors."[32] The LTIC was created by four European investors: Caisse des Dépôts (France), Cassa Depositi e Prestiti (Italy), the European Investment Bank, and KfW (Germany). It has grown to include twenty-three members globally (mainly from G20 countries), and although it acts as a nonlegal, informal platform, the European component through the European Commission (EC) is legally constructed. A steering committee with eight members is responsible for the strategic direction of the LTIC including determining the themes of the annual roundtable. Four of the steering committee members are from the European founding institutions, and the remaining four members are elected from the other international institutions. The secretariat of the LTIC is based in Brussels.

The LTIC organizes an annual conference around a specific theme, bringing together members of the club as well as guests from industry, policy, and academic circles. The main difference of the LTIC is that the members come primarily from government-owned institutions or from development institutions with specific mandates. The program scope may not be quite as large as other initiatives, with a large weighting being placed on how regulation can be enhanced to facilitate long-term investing.

Two initiatives that have come out of the LTIC as a result of collaboration among the founding members are the Marguerite Fund, a pan-European equity fund that aims to act as a catalyst for infrastructure investments implementing key European Union (EU) policies, and InfraMed, an equity fund that focuses on investing in infrastructure projects in the Mediterranean region with a focus on the southern and eastern shores. Both of these initiatives provide examples of reinforced co-operation that the LTIC has been able to facilitate to help support strategic investments and relieve individual government balance sheet burdens.[33]

OECD Long-Term Investment Project

The OECD LTI project was launched in 2012 to help facilitate long-term investment by institutional investors. The primary objective of the project has been to help promote public-private dialogue on the topic of long-term institutional investment. This objective has been facilitated through the development of the G20-OECD High-level Principles on Long-term Investment financing through consultation with institutional investors, government ministries, and other multilateral organizations. The project has also involved coordinating various conferences and meetings including the G20/OECD High-level Roundtable on Institutional Investors and Long-Term Investment, the OECD Infrastructure Summit, and the APEC/OECD Seminar on Institutional Investors and Infrastructure Investment. These conferences have provided a platform for institutional investors from various locations to engage with public-sector officials and other private organizations on the topics of long-term investment and infrastructure financing.

Pacific Pensions Institute

The Pacific Pensions Institute (PPI) is a nonprofit educational organization established in the 1990s with the mission to "assist pension funds, corporations, financial institutions and endowments worldwide with carrying out their fiduciary responsibilities, especially with respect to Asia and the Pacific region." (PPI 2015).

Membership in the PPI is by invitation and capped at 100 member organizations. There are five membership categories for the PPI: investor/asset owner organizations (pension funds, sovereign wealth funds, endowments, foundations, family offices), asset managers/consultancies, individual members with high regard in the institutional investment field, honorary members who have exceptional professional standing, and lifetime members who are recognized for their contribution to PPI.

The organization states that the value proposition stems from both the programs organized for members and the caliber of members themselves. The PPI organizes four annual members-only programs: two roundtables in North America, one roundtable in Asia, and an executive seminar in conjunction with the Asia Roundtable. The programs operate under Chatham House rules (all conversations are off the record) and there is a strict no-marketing rule. Asset owner members are permitted to bring four representatives to each roundtable from the CIO/senior portfolio manager level, whereas asset manager members are entitled to bring two representatives from the CEO/managing director level.

The PPI also includes an Asian Network, comprising pension funds in thirty-three countries throughout Asia and the Pacific. The Asian Network is a partnership with the Asian Development Bank and aims to facilitate discussions around best-practice governance, management, and operational issues for institutional investment management.

Sovereign Investor Institute

The Sovereign Investor Institute (SII) was set up in 2010 as a membership organization of Institutional Investor, the international business-to-business publisher focused on international finance. The parent company of Institutional Investor is the publicly traded international publishing company Euromoney PLC. The SII organizes four roundtables annually rotating among

Asia, Europe, Africa, Latin America, North America and the Middle East for its 360 sovereign fund members represented by eighty-eight countries around the world. In a given year, over two thirds of the membership base participates in the roundtables, which are designed to help the funds engage more actively and productively with government officials, policy makers, academic experts, and senior leaders from the asset management world.

The SII has also launched an online platform to help facilitate collaboration among institutional investors with the eventual aim of being the main portal for formally structuring co-investment deals for investors. Partaking in active scholarship and producing publications and books as part of the roundtables is also a key objective of the SII.

World Economic Forum Global Agenda Council on Long-Term Investing

The World Economic Forum Global Agenda Council on Long-Term Investing, set up in 2010, is an initiative that was born out of the financial crisis to help address long-term investing issues for institutional investors. The council is made up of sixteen members representing senior officials of large institutional investor organizations as well as academics in the institutional investment space.

The council operates as a working group and meets in a roundtable/workshop format to discuss the various issues and challenges associated with long-term investing. The roundtable discussions then contribute to extensive reports and white papers published in conjunction with consultants.

Assessing the Effectiveness of Roundtables and Research Clubs

Largely as a result of the detrimental effects of the financial crisis being exposed and the importance of long-term investment coming to surface, the preceding initiatives have been set up to help raise awareness and facilitate a cooperative effort to address these concerns. The examples provide a selection of the main forums and roundtables that have been developed to specifically attend to the topic of long-term investment by institutional investors.[34] This chapter has proposed that roundtables, member organizations, and research forums can help investors build out their network, which is crucial for facilitating and assisting the investment management process of LTIs. The effectiveness of these gatherings depends on the objectives that the organizers are trying to achieve. Based on the collective experience with attending and helping to organize these meetings, we deduce three main objectives for these types of initiatives.

The first objective of the initiatives is to organize meetings or roundtables that bring a wide range of institutions together with the purpose of facilitating a large networking exercise. In order to achieve this first objective, a wide range of organizations would be invited, including not only asset owners but also asset managers, other private organizations, and government decision makers. In order to facilitate the first objective, a one-to-two-day roundtable that provides a mixture of keynote speakers, panel discussions, special presentations, and breakout sessions along with networking opportunities at coffee and meal breaks would be prepared. Participants may approach these types of roundtables to be lightly informed by the content of the roundtable; however, their main focus would be on capitalizing on connecting with other participants. The nature of these roundtables would perhaps only facilitate introductions, with limited ability to make deeper connections. An intranet or specialized IT service may be set up before the roundtable in order to facilitate the networking exercise.

The second objective of the forums is for participants to actively participate, contribute, and learn from the content of the roundtable. With this second objective, the organizers would go beyond simply asking certain participants to give a presentation at the roundtable and instead ask some or all participants to prepare for the roundtable in a more meaningful way. For example, certain members may be asked to chair a subcommittee that leads to a certain discussion with key outcomes. Another example may be the commitment of members of a forum to contribute significantly to a research paper that comes out of a roundtable or meeting. Continued involvement in these types of forums would be based on the level of contribution and lack of free-riding observed.

The third objective of the roundtables is to build trust and deeper relationships among participants so that formal arrangements such as joint ventures or co-investment vehicles are developed as a result of the meeting. With this third objective, it is likely that only asset owners would be invited to the meetings, as managers or other intermediaries and officials may provide unnecessary distractions to the main focus of the event. The meetings would take place over one or two days, with more time scheduled for setting up side meetings and opportunities to engage with other participants on specific issues or proposals. In order to facilitate this third objective, admittance would be by invitation only and usually hosted at the home location of one of the participants. Buy-in and openness of members to collaboration are necessary prerequisites for these types of gatherings. Success in achieving this third objective will be contingent on the ability to facilitate trust between members. This appears to be the biggest challenge, as trust is usually developed over time and related to similar social attributes such as education, income, occupation, and age (factors outside the control of organizers). Careful design of a program that enables the level of trust between organizations to be enhanced is crucial.

All of these initiatives would incorporate the first two objectives into the planning of the respective meetings taking place. At the time of writing, the Institutional Investor Roundtable was the only forum where asset owners are the sole participants at the organized meetings. All other forums include asset owners as well as other organizations or officials.[35] As a result of their meetings, the World Economic Forum, OECD, LTIC, and PPI produce research papers that are made publicly available, indicating that members must contribute a certain amount of effort. The OECD is able to draw on greater resources, given that producing research reports is a core competency of the underlying organization.

The LTIC and IIR are the only initiatives where co-investment vehicles have been established as a direct result of the relationships developed through the forums. Other partnerships or ventures may have resulted from the other initiatives; however, it is difficult to determine whether the vehicles originated directly from involvement in the roundtables. The insulation of the IIR and LTIC from financial intermediaries in their setup or funding and clear mission/objectives for the forums could be attributed to the success of co-investment platforms being established.

A key consideration that can affect the objectives of the initiatives being achieved is the source of funding used to service the running costs of the organizations/secretariat. A number of the initiatives may have to turn away significant funding sources because of a conflict of interest between what the initiative is trying to achieve and the practices of the organization behind a possible source of funding. For example, asset managers or other intermediaries would see significant benefit in sponsoring these initiatives, as it would provide an excellent opportunity to gain access to potential investors or clients of their business. The IIR, IFSWF, and LTIC would appear to be the only initiatives that are primarily funded independently of financial intermediaries.

Ideally, organizers would target senior executives from the organizations to the roundtables, as this would help draw other high-caliber personnel and presenters. However, while senior executives may help establish high-level relationships between organizations, department managers who work in specific asset classes would be best positioned to help arrange a co-investment relationship or specific deal being arranged with a partner. The personnel most needed to facilitate a formal collaboration with another investor may not have the time available to travel and attend roundtables or meetings with potential collaborators.

This last point leads to the argument for an individual in an investor organization to be solely responsible for facilitating close relationships with other investors around the world. Such an individual, or social capital manager (SCM), would attend international roundtables such as those mentioned earlier but also follow up with any contacts aside from the roundtables to help consolidate and build out the social capital of the organization. An SCM would need to have the breadth and depth of knowledge of the organization's activities to be able to foresee opportunities and connections that could be beneficial for the organization. As indicated by Granovetter's paper "The Strength of Weak Ties" (1973), quite often it is the contacts away from immediate and close circles that can bring the most value to an investor. Having an individual dedicated solely to exploring and developing the weak and strong ties of an organization could reap significant rewards for an investor in the form of new ideas, knowledge, and opportunities.

In sum, this chapter has highlighted some of the initiatives that have been set up to help facilitate the networking and social capital objectives of LTIs. The roundtables and forums introduced here vary in their mission and ability to achieve their objectives; however, many have already provided significant value in facilitating peer-to-peer networking and will continue to evolve along with the objectives of investors and the re-intermediation process. Although this chapter has focused on the horizontal aspect of peer-to-peer collaboration, other types of relationships and new intermediaries may be required to help channel long-term capital vertically into grounded investment opportunities. The vertical aspect of collaboration, which emphasizes the geographic and political embeddedness of social capital, will be addressed in Chapters 4 and 5. Finally, the idea of a designated social capital manager for long-term investor organizations is proposed as a way for LTIs to expand and capitalize on their social capital. Given the theoretical value that building social capital can bring to an investor organization, an SCM could help co-ordinate the network building strategy outlined in this chapter.

3 Re-intermediating Investment Management

One of the clear benefits to LTIs from building their social capital is that they can use this new form of capital to put pressure on their service providers to provide more value. As indicated, the asset management industry has been under pressure to change its operating model, as the asset owners that fund asset managers are increasingly concerned by a growing misalignment of interests. Too often, the value created by external asset managers is captured by the managers rather than flowing through to the asset owners that back them.[1] Worse yet, some managers do not just disproportionately capture the upside, they sometimes also capture upside (in the form of fees) off a portfolio that has none. Many private investment managers actually generate high fee incomes (that investors do not always know about), while producing negative alpha.[2] Much of the poor performance of private-market investment managers has been attributed to a misalignment of interest in governance arrangements between investors and managers.[3] Thus, issues of trust, transparency, and alignment of interest have become key considerations for asset owners globally, and many believe that the investor-manager relationship is in need of new governance arrangements.[4] This raises the question of how such complex relationships can be rearranged to facilitate more alignment of interests.

As indicated in Chapter 1, the second aspect of the re-intermediation thesis recognizes that many investors, because of their size, governance, and regulatory structure, cannot employ the direct investing method or disintermediate asset managers. Investment managers can provide significant value to their investor clients under the right terms and conditions. Re-intermediation, unlike the concept of disintermediation, coheres with this view and is ultimately about understanding how the right terms and conditions can be structured for more alignment between long-term asset owners and managers. This is not necessarily just about reducing the number of links in the chain; it's about thinking critically about how best to make them more efficient and effective. To clarify, the new models being set up as co-investment partnerships, independent of any asset managers, would be considered part of the disintermediation process. However, there are also innovative ways that investors are re-intermediating or structuring their relationships with managers. In this way, the collaborative model combines aspects of disintermediation and re-intermediation. This chapter focuses on re-intermediated governance between investors and asset managers.

Where feasible, we believe that investor-manager relationships should be governed by the principles of relational contracts, which are meant to foster long-term relationships based on mutual dependency, as opposed to short-term discrete classical contracts. We thus propose that investment management contracts should increasingly use relational contracting norms in designing governance arrangements.[5]

Asset Managers and a Lack of Trust

To understand why we need a new framework for looking at investor/manager relationships, it pays to illustrate the full extent of the current problem. The private equity industry perhaps exemplifies the key issues at hand. In particular, the SEC, the IRS, and certain investors are starting to scrutinize irregularities regarding fee income. At the heart of the problem is the fact that certain asset managers have been gaining at the expense of their investors and, although not the focus here, at the expense of taxpayers.

A recent report by the Center for Economic and Policy Research (CEPR) has highlighted how private-equity (PE) general partners have abused their position of power with investors.[6] The authors of the paper find evidence of PE firms "misallocating and inappropriately charging expenses to their investors; ignoring their fiduciary responsibility to pension funds and other investors; manipulating the value of companies in their fund's portfolio; and collecting transaction fees from portfolio companies without registering as 'broker-dealers' as required by law."[7] When it comes to fees and expense practices, PE firms have been found to "double-dip," that is, charge investors for back-office expenses that should have been covered by the 2 percent management fee. They have failed to share monitoring-fee income provided by portfolio companies to the PE firm for consulting and advisory services. Management services agreements signed between PE firms and portfolio companies force companies to pay for annual monitoring fees to the PE firm for ten years despite the firm usually being sold off in a much shorter time frame. Most PE firms also earn fees whenever a transaction is made, which can create misaligned incentives with investors.[8]

PE firms have also been criticized for the way they run their portfolio companies, further indicating the short-term nature and objectives of these actors. A lot of the funding that private-equity firms use to buy companies comes from borrowing large amounts of debt from investment banks, hedge funds, and other alternative lenders. The idea is to improve the efficiency of the companies by bringing in "expert management and techniques" and then selling them for significant profit.[9] Much of this profit, however, often comes from extracting wealth from those companies early on, as indicated by charging various fees, selling company assets, cutting costs, and paying dividends financed from the company's cash flows or from raising additional debt, using the company as collateral.[10] Heavy reliance on debt can make these companies vulnerable to insolvency, if economic climate changes. It can cause them to make poor management decisions, which then makes bankruptcy a strategy where large pension obligations can then be offloaded to government guarantee schemes such as the Pension Benefit Guaranty Corporation. As Lewis (2015) states: "The business model of private equity shifts much of the risk onto the companies they buy. Financial gains go to the Asset Managers, while losses are borne by the companies themselves, including its creditors, and workers and retirees."

While these strategies of PE firms to make as much money as possible as fast as possible may benefit limited-partnership (LP) investors in certain circumstances, they also highlight the misalignment (such as raising debt to pay dividends) for investors wanting to growth their wealth over the long-term through real (ethical) value creation. What has been highlighted is that while LP investors and general-partnership (GP) firms share commercial objectives, the relentless pursuit of profit by GP firms has caused them to act in unethical ways and, in certain circumstances, not in the best interests of their investors. In some instances, these activities violate the terms and conditions of the limited partnership agreement that governs the relationship between investors and managers; in other cases, the wording in the contracts is so vague that it is very hard for investors to do anything about it.[11] The fact that the SEC has started to crack down on some of these practices is evidence that there are problems with the current system. While the SEC has enforced fines (not commensurate with the amount of money that has been taken in fees), it has allowed the parties to pay the fines without admitting guilt.

Clearly, there is a large power asymmetry between the two parties that needs to be evened out. Unfortunately, regulation has not kept pace with the level of distrust. For example, in 2013, a suit filed found two hundred cases of leveraged buyouts where the PE general partner had not been registered as a broker-dealer. Registering as a broker-dealer is required by SEC regulations in order for the firms to be subjected to increased scrutiny and transparency.[12] This is a potential violation of U.S. securities laws. PE firms typically do not provide portfolio company cash flow statements to their investors. An LP investor could theoretically sue for more detailed information, but that would compromise the investor's ability to invest in future funds.[13] Against this backdrop, this chapter aims to understand in more detail how the current situation has arisen and recommend improvements to the system.

Organizational Theory—Employment Versus Service Contracts for Investment Management

Before analyzing governance arrangements between investors and their managers, we must first provide insight into the generic decision-making process for institutional investors. Clark and Monk (2013) relate the question of insourcing and outsourcing of investment management to a choice between directly employing investment managers in house or entering into service contracts with third-party providers on a fee-for-service basis (employment or service contracts). This stems from the seminal work on the nature of the firm by Coase (1937), in which the question of managing production in-house or to outsource and subcontract activities is related to the make-or-buy decision. More recently, scholars have related the make-or-buy decision to issues of governance and hierarchy, which have relationship implications.[14] If the make option is selected, governance is internal and conducted through hierarchy. Relationships are based on hierarchical control, authority, and power. If the buy option is chosen, then the types of external contract frame governance.[15] The types of buy or service contracts have been analyzed by using a spectrum of contracts (discussed further in the next section) based on transaction cost analysis and sociology theory.[16]

Clark and Monk (2013) discuss the difficulty in setting standardized employment contracts across an investor organization where noninvestment employees provide accounting, actuarial, and custodial services (which are needed regardless of market conditions). They also distinguish the factors that may contribute to appraising investment talent in transparent asset classes compared with opaque assets. In transparent asset classes, they believe it is easier to differentiate between luck and skill, whereas in opaque asset classes, higher rewards could accrue to managers without knowing exactly where the source of return may have come from.

Smaller institutions that are unable to in-source the various tasks that make up an investment strategy are forced to engage in service contracts with external investment managers. Service contracts with outsourced managers stipulate the target rate of return, related costs, and mechanisms for renewing or terminating the contract in the future.[17] Clark and Monk (2013) differentiate between investment management bilateral service contracts used for public-market investing, which can be terminated at will, and contracts in pooled investment vehicles, which are more common in private-market investing. In the latter arrangement, the terms of the contract may be different for different parties, with larger, earlier, and more sophisticated investors of capital gaining more favorable terms such as discount on costs, private briefings, and direct engagement on issues of relevance. Smaller clients thus face larger costs; know little about the products, organization, or performance of external managers; and are likely to come late (if at all) to the successful managers and stay longer with managers whose performance has diminished.[18]

Service contracts with external investment managers act as the governance mechanism for determining how the costs and benefits of the investment management process are distributed between principal investors and their agents (fund managers). Studying how the contracts are conceptually defined enables insights not only into the details of the agreement but also into the behaviors adopted by the parties.

Contract Theory: Transaction Cost Analysis

Contract theory provides a framework for addressing the principal-agent issues in investment management service contracts and provides possible answers for an improved way of governing the relationship between investors and their managers. Grounded in law and economics, contract theory looks at the decision-making process of individuals and businesses under uncertain conditions or when there is asymmetric information on economic exchanges and transactions.[19] In legal scholarship and subsequently through transaction cost theory in economics, a continuum of contracts has been developed to facilitate an understanding of various human exchanges.[20] A three-way discussion of contracts described by scholars such as Macneil and Williamson (1979) shows that contracts are varied and the governance structures within which transactions are executed must be adapted for the particular nature of the transaction.[21]

First, the classical law of contract stems from the nineteenth century and is used to model one-off, discrete and self-contained transactions. In classical contracts, the identity of parties to the transaction are considered irrelevant, the terms and limits of the agreement are carefully outlined, and the remedies are narrowly prescribed, predictable, and not open-ended. Such a situation corresponds to the "ideal" market transaction in economics: "of short duration, involving limited personal interactions, and with precise party measurements of easily measured objects of exchange."[22] Classical contracts place a large emphasis on price in the arrangement, based on the absence of relationship recognition. Price essentially determines how the transaction is governed.[23]

Second, in recognition that a completely discrete transaction is a near impossibility, Williamson formulated a hybrid form of *neoclassical* contract, which is based on the existence of transaction costs and provides an alternative contracting relation or governance structure in situations where the discrete or classical model of contract breaks down.[24] These "transaction-cost" contracts are based on the realization that the world is complex, that agreements are incomplete, and that some contracts will never be reached unless the settlement machinery provides confidence to both parties.[25] Third-party assistance for resolving disputes in the form of arbitration as opposed to litigation is a feature of neoclassical contract. This is common in construction projects, which are rarely structured as single exchanges and comprise a series of stage payments, each carrying transaction cost, albeit flowing from a single contract.[26]

Third, relational contracts, at the far end of the spectrum, are characterized by long duration and personal involvement by the parties and are viewed as relations rather than as discrete transactions.[27] The increased duration and complexity of certain contracts could not completely be covered by the neo-classical adjustment-contract concept, which has led to the introduction of relational contracts. In contrast to classical and transaction-cost contracts, relational contracts have as a reference point for effecting adaptations in the agreement the actual relation as it has developed over time.[28] The planning for relational contracts is more often tentative rather than binding and focuses on planning the structures and processes to govern the relation in the future.[29] Macneil uses the concept of *relational* in two ways when describing these forms of exchange.[30] The first use of *relational* refers to the fact that "all contracts occur in the context of a social matrix" and consideration must be given to societal and political influences on the exchange.[31] The second use of *relational* for contract theory refers to the fact that "many contracts involve a continuing relationship between the parties, which will affect the way in which their contract operates."[32] Relational contracts have been described as self-enforcing agreements in repeated interactions with cooperation in the present, contingent on the expectations of future exchanges. They can be formal or informal agreements sustained by the value of future relationships, connecting actors over time and space where there is reciprocity and repeated linkages, capturing the process of transacting as opposed to a discrete transaction.[33] Trust in these relational contracts is dependent on the trustworthy status over time through repeated exchange.[34] Just as trust is crucial for promises made between people, trust in relational contracts may be the product of some previous acquaintance with a person, or based on impressions of the respective personalities in the framework of ongoing relationships.[35] Table 3.1 summarizes the three categories of contracts.

Proponents of relational theory argue that generic contracts are only as good as the relationships they create.[36] A social orientation and sociopsychological contract is more likely to induce decisions in the interest of a client despite seeming irrational from an economic perspective.[37] When unpacked at the level of the exchange, the structure and quality of relationships have a major influence on the value created. Relational contracts require norms of obligation and cooperation to coordinate the exchange. Macneil (1974) proposes the following contractual norms or behavioral patterns for relational contracts: role integrity, reciprocity, implementation of planning, effectuation of consent, flexibility, contractual solidarity, restitution, reliance and expectation interests, creation and restraint of power, propriety of means, and

TABLE 3.1 Classification of service contracts

Classical contracts	*Neo-classical contracts*	*Relational contracts*
"One-off," short term, discrete transactions	Alternative to classical	Longer-term
Identity of parties irrelevant	"Nonideal," transaction costs	Process of transacting as opposed to discrete transaction
Terms and limits carefully outlined	More emphasis on third-party assistance, not litigation	Planning is tentative, not binding
"Ideal" market transaction	For more complex situations where parties gain confidence from settlement machinery	Repeated exchanges, based on trust, cooperation and mutual dependency
Large emphasis on price	—	Personal involvement of parties is important
Example: Certain limited partnership agreements (LPAs)	**Example:** Construction projects (a series of stage payments flowing from a single contract)	**Example:** Investment management agreements (IMAs), managed accounts, funds-of-one

SOURCE: Williamson 1979, MacNeil 1977.

harmonization.[38] These norms of relational contracting have been extended by scholars and utilized in various applications, for example in civil infrastructure projects and other interorganizational collaborations.[39]

In a survey conducted on the travel industry to illustrate business-to-business marketing relationships in service industries, Schakett and colleagues (2011) found that service quality was only 27 percent attributable to economic bonds (exchange and transaction), 36 percent to a structural bond (contractual), and 44 percent attributable to social bond (norms and social contracts), pointing toward the importance of relationships. Smyth (2014), drawing on a quote from Nahapiet and colleagues (2005:4), states that "the economy is also a relational economy since the structure and quality of relationships are a major influence both on the creation and exploitation of knowledge." The prominence of relations in the knowledge economy is even more apparent in the interdependent service economy.[40]

This chapter thus proposes the relational contracting method as a more suitable contracting conceptual framework for approaching the investor–fund manager relationship. However, just as a purely discrete transaction is practically impossible, it is unlikely that a pure relational contract actually exists. The spectrum of contracts outlined here, despite being idealistic in nature, provides a useful theoretical framework for understanding how and why the practices in investment management have been carried out. As Faulconbridge and colleagues (2007), drawing on Swedberg (2000:193–194) and Weber (1978:3), state: "the categories should be understood as theoretical conceptualisations of a complex and layered social reality which allow us to focus on the discrepancies between the two—ideal type and empirical observations." Consequently, we now look at how the relational contracting *concept* can be applied to the investment management setting.

Re-intermediated Investment Contracts: From Discrete to Relational

The perfect tender model, or discrete contract, presumes the existence of a complete contract covering all possible contingencies.[41] In the event of nonperformance or deviation, discrete contracts assume that the consequences are relatively predictable from the beginning and are not open-ended. However, with most investment relationships, mistakes are made, parties' interests are obscured in details, and not all possible contingencies are foreseen. In the case of private-market investing, where long-term contracts are executed under conditions of uncertainty, "complete presentiation"[42] under discrete contracts is almost impossible.[43] Equally problematic is the fact that trust is a fundamental driver of success in long-term-investment relationships. Overly formal contracts, however, may signal distrust with an exchange partner, and instead of discouraging, may encourage opportunistic behavior in the relationship.[44]

Based on the behavior of certain managers, the traditional limited partnership or fund model typically used by investment managers to raise capital from investors to invest in private-market assets seems to have adopted the characteristics of a classical, discrete form of contractual governance. The limited partnership, as shown in Figure 3.1, is structured by a manager that controls the general partner (GP) of the fund and is charged with making all of the investment and management decisions for the fund. Institutional investors buy interests into the partnership as limited partners. Limited partners (LPs) have limited liability and have no control over the daily management of the fund. A number of terms are usually stipulated in the legal limited partnership agreement (LPA) between LPs and the manager, including the

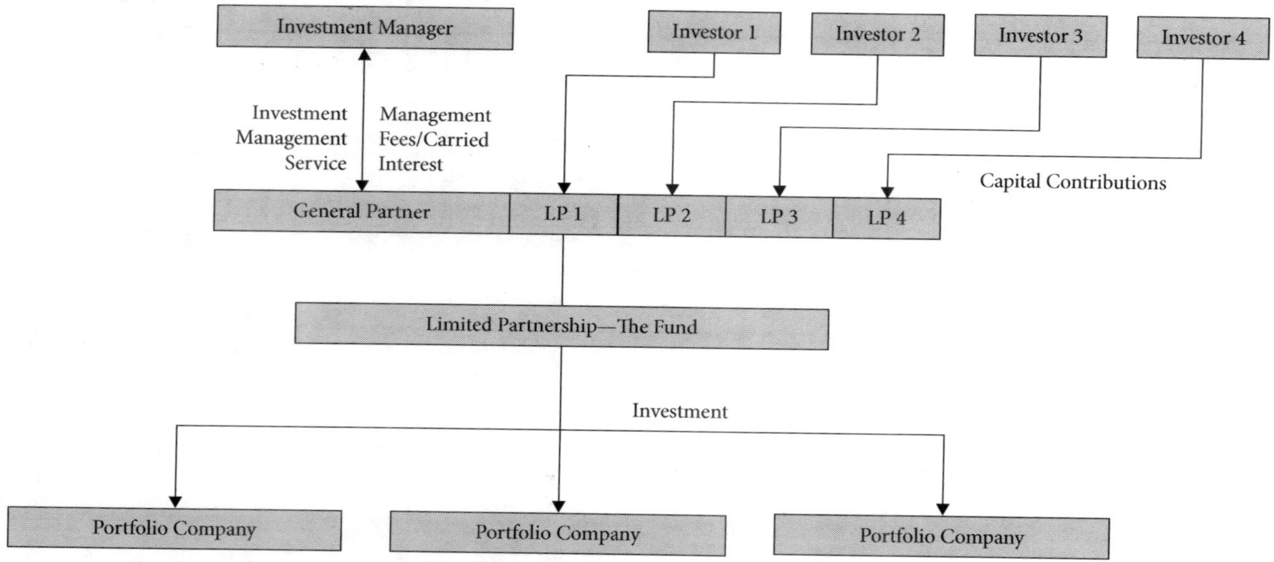

FIGURE 3.1 Limited partnership “fund” structure

target IRR (internal rate of return, or investment performance), the hurdle rate (the IRR that a fund must achieve before the manager or GPs may receive a share of the profits of the fund), carried interest (share of the profits that a GP receives after returning the required capital to investors), and the key man clause (if a specified member of the management team ceases to spend a specified amount of time on the partnership, the manager is temporarily suspended from making any new investments). Committed capital is the legally binding amount of money committed during the fund-raising process, and it generally cannot change once a fund has been launched. Committed capital is drawn over time as the partnership calls capital to make investments. Management fees are paid ostensibly annually to the GP to cover salaries and overhead costs and are calculated as a percentage of total committed capital or total invested capital.[45]

Limited partners usually do not have any approval rights over investments, with the decision lying solely with the GP. After an investment is made, GPs often prepare a special announcement for their LPs, followed by an information memorandum describing the investment. Ongoing communication between the GP and LP varies but usually includes reporting packages quarterly or semiannually to provide updates on the performance of the fund's investment.

Despite the idiosyncratic, long-term nature and large amounts of capital being transferred, the arrangement between institutional investors and fund managers through the limited partnership or fund model can be likened to a classical, discrete contract where the identity of parties is irrelevant and there is a strong emphasis on price as the governance mechanism. The LPA binds the LPs and the GP together, and the relationship is essentially governed solely by the terms set out in the fund documents, which it would seem are not always adhered to. The investor then has very limited involvement in the management of the fund: advisory boards do not generally have much power and investors cannot easily move their assets out of the fund.

Certain relational elements are involved in drawing up LPAs between LPs and GPs. For example, certain fiduciary duties are implied outside the common-law governing provisions in these arrangements, and in many cases relationships have been formed between investors and managers. However, given the practices of certain asset managers, specifically the clear examples of abuses of power highlighted earlier, LPAs have often been constructed with a clear weighting toward classical, discrete contracts rather than mutually dependent, cooperative and transparent relational contracts. Some LPAs specifically state that asset managers may waive their fiduciary responsibility toward their limited partners. This indicates that the GP can make decisions that maximize the fund's profits, even if those decisions detrimentally affect the LP investors. This has serious implications for pension funds and other institutional investors that have fiduciary obligations to their own members and clients. They would be in breach of their fiduciary obligations if they are letting asset managers put their own interests ahead of the LPs.

We thus propose that a shift toward relational contracting should continue to occur for delegated institutional investment into private markets. We believe that the art of asset management should not be about writing a contract that seems reasonable on the surface while hiding unreasonable payouts and behavior. However, as stated earlier, arriving at a purely relational form of governance may not be a reasonable assertion.

The implementation issues of relational governance have been widely discussed in the theory of contract by both economics and management scholars. Within economics, a central contribution is that of Baker and colleagues (2002), who illustrate the difference between formal and relational contracts and the importance of the latter for understanding informal organizational processes within firms. More recent work has looked at the theoretical interplay between formal and relational mechanisms identifying both substitutive and complementary roles between the two.[46] The relevant management literature presents empirical findings on the contracting modes in different settings.[47]

Quite often, it is assumed that a relationship based on trust reduces transaction costs by "replacing contracts with handshakes."[48] Generally speaking, increases in formal contractual complexity discourage the formation of relational governance, whereas increases in relational governance discourage the use of complex contracts.[49] Despite this, however, when repercussions or hazards are severe, the combination of formal and informal safeguards may deliver greater exchange performance than either governance choice in isolation.[50] Indeed, Poppo and Zenger (2002) state:

> The presence of clearly articulated contractual terms, remedies and processes of dispute resolution as well as relational norms of flexibility, solidarity, bilateralism, and continuance may inspire confidence to co-operate in inter-organisational exchanges.

This sentiment, implying a combination of formal and relational form of contract, provides the conceptual framework for the proposed re-intermediated governance of investment management relationships. In the investor-manager relationship, the explicit outlay of fees and other terms and conditions in the investment contract needs to be accompanied by a relational form of governance that is based on trust, reciprocity, and repeated exchange. This may already happen in certain circumstances, but in many others, as indicated by the SEC investigations of PE firms, it does not. The formal element of re-intermediated contracts should specify detailed schedules of roles and responsibilities as opposed to just detailed schedules disclaiming liability. Developing trust would require being in constant dialogue with investors, to go above and beyond the bare requirements of the formal contractual terms. Clear communication of key issues, such as fines, ESG factors, market trends, and tax issues, would also help build confidence for investors so that shocks or variable performance can be contextualized and rationalized. We emphasize here the importance of transparency, which has been shown to be lacking in certain investment management agreements. An increase in transparency will help build trust between investors and managers in even the most formal limited partnership agreements, where developing personalized relationships with all investors can be difficult.[51]

In the investment management industry, considerable uncertainty is involved with how decisions are made and performance achieved. Empirical work indicates that in cases of greater uncertainty, a relational, more flexible arrangement in the contract leads to more value.[52] The relational value of solidarity becomes particularly important in promoting exchange into the future when conflicts may arise and the adaptive limits of formal contracts become exhausted.[53] Adjudication is an important consideration with relational contracts given their incomplete nature. The exact arrangement will depend on the situation; however, third-party arbitration for disputes, as described by neoclassical contracts, would be more likely and appropriate in this setting as opposed to formal judicial procedures, given the large amounts of capital at play and the reluctance of both parties to have high-profile lawsuits.

Relational governance may also promote the implementation of formal contracts. As a close relationship is developed or sustained (such as between two institutional investors for a co-investment relationship), contracts are used to formalize the arrangement, or revisions to existing contracts can be made to reflect prior experiences.[54] What does this mean in practice for fund managers? While the specific terms and conditions of funds written into the formal contract will differ for different asset classes, some general principles can be applied.

Take as a case study for this chapter the infrastructure asset class, for which fees have become a contentious issue and trust and long-term orientation is crucial. There is now greater appreciation of the diversity of risk/return profiles of infrastructure assets, and this should be reflected in the fees charged to investors. It is understandable that a fund investing in greenfield assets in the emerging markets carrying greater risk will charge a higher fee compared to a fund investing in brownfield assets in developed countries. Various developments in fee structure have taken place as a result of the market adjusting for differing opinions. It is widely perceived that management fees should just cover the cost of running the fund on a day-to-day basis as opposed to providing a source of profit for the manager. Given the large size of funds, a 2 percent management fee, common for private-equity funds, is considered too high, particularly for brownfield, core economic infrastructure assets in OECD countries.[55] A key consideration here is whether the total fee and portfolio construction costs for an investor are greater than the illiquidity and risk premium of investing in these assets.

Performance fees are usually based on a hurdle rate and carried interest. Similarly, the hurdle rate will depend on the strategy employed and should be different for brownfield infrastructure assets in developed countries compared with development projects in emerging economies. Managers should earn a performance fee only if it is adding value (or generating alpha).[56] One of the ongoing difficulties in determining an appropriate fee structure for infrastructure funds is the holding period for investments. Unlike private equity, where the typical holding period is four or five years, infrastructure investments should perhaps be held for ten years or more, with many investors' preferences moving toward even longer holding periods. The shorter-term focus of private-equity funds is more suited to turnaround or development deals, and the mandatory exit is not consistent with the long-term-hold philosophy of core infrastructure. Contributions, valuations, and liquidity are all controlled at the manager's discretion, and distributions are only made toward the end of the fund life.[57]

Relational infrastructure contracts would be more suited to open-end funds or funds of length greater than fifteen years, as this would be more appropriately matched to the long-term liabilities of institutional investors and more suited to developing the type of partnership required. Open-end funds have an ongoing investment period and provide immediate exposure to income-generating assets (rather than a blind pool fund). With open-end funds, there is greater ability to grow and diversify the fund over time and no rush to deploy capital. With regard to contributions, investors have more control, valuations are regular and independent, and liquidity is available from cash yield with the option of exits and redemption if appropriate. Investors also have control over reinvestment and distribution decisions.[58]

The exact terms and conditions of the formal part of the investor-fund manager contract will depend on the types of assets invested into. However, a relational form of governance should complement the formal aspect of the contract. This involves creating a deeper relationship with investors to help build trust by having regular dialogue and facilitating more fluid, transparent information flows between the parties (without compromising the ability of the manager to carry out its function effectively).

Practical Considerations and Barriers to Relational Contracts

Historical Context and Relational Governance

Historically, institutional investors appointed investment managers to provide advisory and discretionary management services using tailored investment management agreements (IMAs). Under these more relational agreements, the investor was the client and the investment manager was the service provider. The purpose of the relationship was to provide services to the client. However, as institutional investors started to allocate more capital into private and alternative asset classes,[59] investment managers started to employ the limited partnership or fund model. The funds were established as standalone businesses, which sought passive capital from investors. The purpose of the relationship was to provide capital for the investment manager to run its business. In the United States, private-equity funds were excluded from coverage by the Investment Company Act of 1940, which requires the disclosure of financial policies, limits the amount of leverage, and requires a board with a large number of independent members.[60] Investors accepted the model as they had little experience in alternative assets and private markets. An asset manager typically presents the same LP agreement to an investor that it has signed in the past, which puts the burden of proof on investors to explain why what they agreed to before doesn't work now.[61] Asset managers tend to market the same terms and conditions to other investors to intensify the pressure among investors to sign the agreement or be left out. The lack of transparency surrounding asset manager practices and the confidentiality requirements in LPAs have protected asset managers from public scrutiny. This behavior seems to have continued following the financial crisis, although as investors have slowly grown in size, sophistication, and bargaining power, the default fund model is coming under scrutiny.

Reverting to the offering of managed accounts or funds of one would enable a more personal relationship to be developed between investor and manager, where not only better terms and conditions are provided to investors, but an overall better duty of care is given, including frequent communication and greater transparency. The formal terms of a specialized managed account, including compensation, termination, and duration, can be negotiated to reflect both parties' interests a lot more easily.

Managed accounts also allow decision makers of institutional investor organizations to more effectively monitor the activities of fund managers, and greater transparency enables them to demonstrate to their own stakeholders that they are doing so. The application of relational contracting principles and norms in these situations would be easier and more likely to lead to success for the parties involved. A movement toward discretionary IMAs with fund managers, adapting to allow investors to appoint them on this basis rather than invest in a fund, is part of the proposed re-intermediated model of relational investing we describe shortly.

Within the limited partnership or fund structure, the differentiated investor base entering into the arrangement makes blanket relational offerings challenging. Larger and earlier investors are given better treatment by managers through lower fees, and greater information disclosure, which makes it harder for smaller investors to get access to the better managers. The creation of investor-led platforms that adapt the fund model may provide a solution to this problem to help smaller investors get access to private-market opportunities in a more aligned way. The importance of developing a wide network is crucial for these smaller investors when their inclusion by the top-performing managers and sophisticated investors is purely discretionary. As indicated earlier for core economic infrastructure, certain aspects of the terms of a limited partnership agreement can be revised to ensure more alignment for investors that must use the fund model to access opportunities.

Investor Control Versus Decision-Making Power

An issue that seems to surface when talking about investor control is the difference between governance and investment decision-making power. We believe that investors can have governance, while the investment manager has full discretionary management power. Managers may wrongly think that governance means that the investors would be able to retrospectively second-guess their investment decisions. A clear distinction needs to be made between process (which the investors can criticize, and which the investment managers should be obligated to comply with and accountable if they do not) and judgment/discretion (which is binding on all parties). Partnership between investors and investment managers is about combining governance (including investor control and accountability) with discretionary investment power on the part of the manager.

There can be disadvantages to investors having too much control in their investments. In the corporate governance context, scholars such as Bainbridge and Arrow argue that shareholder activism, where institutional investors review management decisions and step in when management performance falters, does not differ from giving investors the power to make management decisions in the first place.[62] They believe that preserving managerial discretion should always be the default presumption to ensure efficiency.

Also, too much investor control can be crippling to the investment management process, particularly when there are multiple investors with heterogeneous preferences. Greater rights for investors to facilitate a relational form of governance may thus only be appropriate in funds of one (which have a sole investor in a fund) and separate managed-account scenarios where specific, tailor-made investment management agreements would be appropriate. Investors would need to understand the requirements of having greater control and responsibility over their delegated investment decisions. This means having processes to robustly appraise the fees and costs of the financial products they are investing into as well as the bandwidth and resources to monitor the underlying investments that managers have made on their behalf. The greater surveillance would be designed not to impede the managers' ability to carry out their function but to help ensure that investors know exactly what they are investing into and the costs of doing so. In many ways, this would be a requirement for them to be appropriately carrying out the fiduciary obligation to their members and clients.

In summary, greater scrutiny over fees, costs, and process would be required by investors in all arrangements with managers. Larger, more sophisticated investors should take greater responsibility and control over investments when engaging in co-investments, funds of one, or separate managed accounts.

Incentivizing Managers

From a practical viewpoint, a relational perspective means redefining the terms and conditions of the agreement to include more transparency and collaboration between investor and manager. This may involve increasing the time horizon of the funds, or making them open-ended with the ability to withdraw capital under certain rules or conditions. The subject of fees is perhaps the biggest point of contention when designing the commercial contract for delegated investing. This is partly because fees in a contract need to be tied to a predetermined formula, and any situation is open to being gamed by a manager. Of particular concern is the inability to design a contract where the investor has the option of paying the manager as much as it thinks the manager is worth for a particular year, given all other factors and assessing the appropriateness of the investment decision at the time it was made.[63]

Calculating management fees by referring to a fixed formula generally distorts manager behavior. If they are based on invested capital, the manager has the incentive to invest the money as quickly as possible; if they are based on committed capital, the manager can arguably be paid for doing very little. If a fund performs very badly, where the likelihood of beating the hurdle rate is very low, a zombie fund may emerge in which the manager has no incentive to exit investments at all. If performance fees are based on carry, the manager has the incentive to sell the asset as quickly as possible in order to release the carry, which is often calculated according to IRR calculations dependent on time as a critical factor. Similarly, rewarding managers for outperformance may encourage excessive risk taking, which may be inappropriate for certain asset classes (such as infrastructure), particularly since there is already a built-in incentive for managers to seek high returns as they generally need to establish historic outperformance in order to raise future funds.

Ideally, a contract would be designed so that a significant part of a manager's remuneration is discretionary. This is a lot easier to achieve with employment contracts as opposed to service contracts, where, for example, a manager directly employed by an investor can have a bonus assessed on the appropriateness of their investment decisions in the context of the investment environment in which they were made. One solution might be to have a performance fee "bank," where a manager may earn high performance fees but the money goes in a bank and what is paid in any year is limited to some sort of maximum as a function of assets or base fee. This way, a manager who has one good year followed by five poorly performing years can use what is in the bank to reverse the original number.

Incentives are generally based on reward and punishment (the carrot and the stick). However, the focus in investment management has generally been solely on the reward aspect of incentivization, with the effect that fees have been increased, without due consideration being given to the possibility of punishing managers for behavior that the investor does not deem to be in their interest. The industry often justifies high levels of carried interest by arguing that in the absence of such rewards, the managers might be tempted to simply take the management fees on committed capital and pay little attention to investing the fund in the interests of the asset owners. This approach fails to give sufficient regard to the other aspect of incentivization, which is the fear of punishment. In many funds currently on the market, it is difficult if not impossible to remove an underperforming or otherwise unsatisfactory manager. If the termination provisions in fund documents were more robust, this could provide a less expensive way of incentivizing managers to act in the interests of investors.

First, most "no-fault divorce" clauses (permission to remove a manager outside formal breaches of the contract) can be triggered only by a large majority of investors. This means that at least 75 percent of investors need to agree on (a) replacement being appropriate, (b) how to fund the legal action necessary, and (c) what to replace the current manager with. This can be difficult, particularly when managers have received commitments from a diverse range of investors that do not know each other and have different priorities.

Second, most termination-for-cause provisions require a lower majority of votes (usually a bare majority), but cause is narrowly defined in most funds, making it nearly impossible to prove. Many funds require a nonappealable court decision to trigger termination for cause, which means the investors would need to go all the way to the highest court (by which time the fund would probably have terminated in any event).

Finally, many funds have extremely high break fees, where the relationship is terminated without cause (no-fault divorce), which makes it prohibitively expensive to remove a manager.

If investors were able to negotiate exit provisions more robustly, it would have a significant impact on the attitude of investment managers toward their investors.[64] At present, the only real discipline to go with the fee/carry incentive is the prospect of investors not committing capital in future fundraisings, which doesn't appear to have much impact. A more relational form of governance between investors and managers may involve reduced reliance on incentivizing through high fee/carried interest, and instead focus on developing more robust termination clauses in the limited partnership agreement.

Other Practical Barriers to Relational Governance

While the relational contracting idea provides guidance for improving the arrangement between investors and investment managers in the investment management process, there may be limitations in the practical implementation of the concept.

The first barrier is the fact that any attempt to wrest control away from the investment management industry will face strong resistance. Asset managers threaten to end the relationship with LPs if they publicize the fee and expense structures in LPAs. An example of this was when the Iowa public pension fund received a public-records request regarding the fees it paid to private-equity firms. One of their PE firms, Kohlberg, Kravis and Roberts (KKR), indicated that making the information public could "jeopardize" its access to further opportunities.[65] The industry has developed sizable resources, which it can use to defend its lucrative rents. It would appear that there is too much money being extracted as fees and carry to expect the investment management industry to willingly move toward a fairer, trust-based approach. The number of agents in the investment chain makes it easier for the investment management industry to break down the weakest links to prevent change. Intermediation is self-perpetuating in that the chain of intermediaries makes it easier to resist change and disintermediation.

Another barrier to change is the language of fund management. For example, the *GP* and *LP* monikers have come to mean *investment manager* and *investor* across the industry. The terms *general partner* and *limited partner* are legal shorthand terms that attach a number of rights, liabilities, and obligations to each party (with all decision-making power being given to GPs), and the language itself may not be helping change. The International Limited Partners Association (ILPA), for example, in many ways, is handing over control to investment managers by simply including *limited partners* in its own organizational name. If the industry were able to remove these titles and instead refer to the functions as *investment managers* and *investors*, that in itself could create a conceptual space to renegotiate the relationships between the parties.

A third barrier is the investment consultant that sits between investors and investment managers. Investment consultants also extract rents from the system by preventing managers from developing relationships directly with the investors. The amount of assets controlled by these consultants worldwide makes it difficult for investment managers to be seen to be challenging them or encroaching on their territory in any way.[66] Investors should employ the services of consultants in the role of advisors as opposed to gatekeepers.

Summary

A re-intermediation process is needed to redefine the relationship between asset owners and managers for deploying capital into private-market asset classes. In many ways, this chapter explains some of the trends that are already occurring in the industry. It provides a theoretical illustration of why certain behavior has occurred as it has, and some theoretically backed solutions for how the situation can be improved. Based on theory and practice, we have come up with some guidelines for relational investing:

First, we believe that large asset owners (with assets of more than $15 billion)[67] should take advantage of their scale and time horizon by pushing for *discrete mandates*; that is, they should design purpose-built IMAs to form partnerships with managers in the form of separate managed accounts, funds of one, or co-investments with their managers. The partnerships should be based on trust and mutual dependency but also have the formal terms and conditions agreed upon in an appropriate fashion, based on the characteristics of the investments and investors.

Generally speaking, the larger asset owners should be pursuing greater *control*. These investors, when appropriate, should take on greater responsibility for the success or failure of investments by moving closer (in terms of intermediaries) to the underlying assets and working alongside managers. As control is shifted, resources will also have to shift.

All investors, including smaller asset owners (with assets of less than $15 billion), should seek greater *transparency.* All investors should ensure full transparency in the LPA over fees being charged by the asset manager (expenses should be fully disclosed, asset valuations independently made, other fees associated with portfolio company investments fully disclosed, and conflicts of interest reduced).

All investors should also scrutinize incentives, including *termination.* The clauses for termination in LPAs should be robustly negotiated to enable accountability without enabling short-term distortions. Profit-based incentives should be capped in a way that investors can reward managers based on the context in which investment decisions are made. A "fee bank" idea could provide a solution here.

For many asset owners, achieving these principles may mean reducing the number of managers in their portfolio. This consolidation may help ensure that sufficient resources are used to form relational partnerships with managers. However, because of the extra responsibilities of investors associated with relationally contracting managers, it may not be practical for an investor organization to have these arrangements for all of their manager relationships, which could include 50 to 100 or many more managers, depending on the size of the investor.

Figure 3.2 summarizes the discussion in this chapter on the re-intermediation of investment managers using the relational contracting concept. As Figure 3.2 illustrates, both investors and investment managers should approach the investment management process with the ideals of relational contracting in mind. Depending on the type of investor, the formal aspect of the arrangement will be either an IMA or an LPA. In the case of an LPA, attention should be focused on transparency and negotiating robust termination clauses as opposed to having high fees or carried interest as the incentive for good performance.

While a lot of the focus from this discussion of relational governance has been placed on investment managers, investors will also need to play a role to facilitate a successful relationship. Greater responsibility will be placed on investors to help forge successful partnerships with their managers, particularly if greater control and scrutiny of investments are desired. Part of the

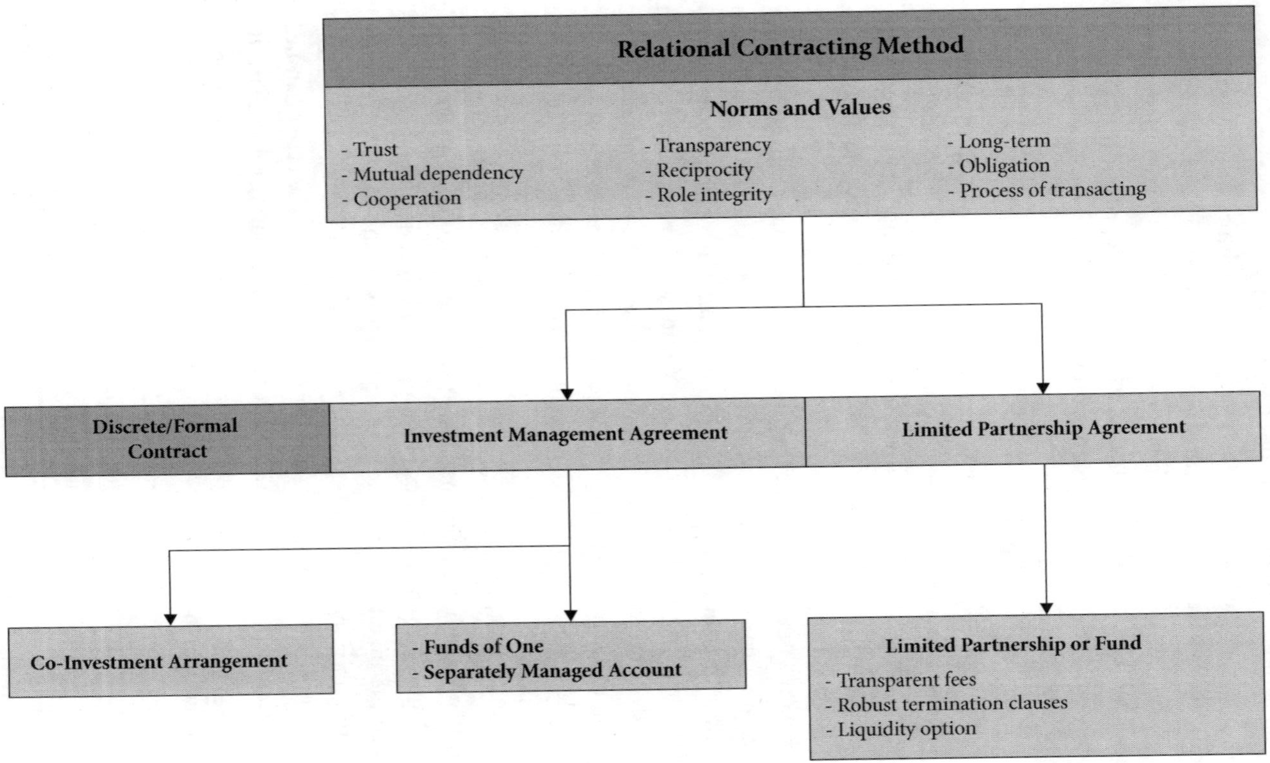

FIGURE 3.2 Re-intermediation with investment managers summary diagram

reason why some managers have continued with dubious practices is a lack of oversight and interest shown by investors. There can be drawbacks with greater investor control, but at the very least, investors should demand complete transparency on the fees and costs they are exposed to. In January 2016, the ILPA released a template for standardizing reporting of fees, expenses, and carried interest. While this is a step in the right direction, the adoption of its use is voluntary. A number of investors and asset managers have publicly endorsed the template, although it is unclear whether they will adopt it. A combined, conscious effort by investors to stand up to their asset managers and regulators to ensure that there are adequate enforcements will help police manager behavior and protect the interests of investors and their fiduciaries.

This chapter also highlights the importance of legal services and raises the question of whether investors should establish their own legal services so that they can be informed consumers of the contract binding them with managers. Currently, in-house legal services (if they have them) are most often used to procure external legal services and hold them accountable. Should they be doing more? In the same way that asset owners need to attract the finest investment talent, should they also be looking to attract the brightest legal talent? How will they ensure that their own legal services are sensitive to the investment goals and objectives of the institution?

4 New Vehicles to Drive the Collaborative Model

IN CHAPTER 2, WE ILLUSTRATED the importance of a networking strategy for long-term investors and indicated that co-investing with trusted investment partners was one of the ultimate objectives of a collaboration strategy. Investors are increasingly using the co-investment method to access assets on more favorable terms, either through an option tied to an existing external fund manager or through an investor-led platform that collates peer investors together.

The performance of co-investment among asset managers and their investors has been studied, revealing outcomes that can best be described as "mixed."[1] But peer co-investment vehicles, joint ventures, and platform companies led by investors have been underresearched, which is why these methods for accessing assets are looked at here. These new partnerships have been developed to pool capital in a more aligned way and to form specific vehicles for accessing an attractive investment area. The World Economic Forum has loosely defined co-investment vehicles, joint ventures, and platforms under the partnership model of direct investing and predicted that these types of arrangements are likely to increase in the future.[2]

Co-Investment Methods

In recent years, the academic studies that have illustrated the potential benefits of direct investing over traditional fund investing[3] identified three methods of private-market investing along a spectrum of dependency on intermediaries: traditional fund investing, co-investing, and direct investing. The co-investment method illustrated in these studies is related to the method whereby an institutional investor is offered the option to invest alongside a fund manager in addition to investing in the fund, as illustrated in Figure 4.1. The reliance of the investor on the GP (fund manager) is still very apparent for this method of investing.

The co-investment method of investing, illustrated in Figure 4.1, has provided an alternative for investors to access investment opportunities on more favorable terms compared with the fund model. Co-investments have been prevalent in the private-equity asset class and are an increasing feature of infrastructure fund offerings. A survey conducted by Probitas Partners in October 2013 showed that out of the 137 institutional investors participating, 35 percent now have co-investment strategies for private equity, up from 22 percent when the same survey was conducted two years prior. From the Palico Marketplace database, more than 20 percent of all U.S. buyout transactions undertaken since 2009 involved co-investments compared with less than 5 percent of buyouts for the same five-year period leading up to 2008.

Despite the uptake, and while direct investments have indicated better performance, the academic literature has been mixed in the analysis of performance of investors making co-investments alongside fund investments. In particular, Fang and colleagues (2015), using data on seven large institutional investors over 20 years, showed that co-investments underperform traditional fund investments. Notwithstanding possible bias in the study (due to the co-investment deals being substantially larger than the fund investments), the authors explain why co-investments offered by fund managers may not perform as well.

First, an adverse selection problem exists where fund managers may offer lower-quality deals for co-investments. With co-investments, fund managers relinquish a large portion of their management and performance fees and therefore may lack the incentive to bring their best deals to investors for co-investments. In terms of asset management, fund managers may have a lower motivation to maximize the value created in co-invested firms, spending more time on the investments that will earn greater fees. As depicted by Figure 4.2 (based on a Preqin survey of 140 private equity LPs[4]), co-investments can be onerous for fund managers by hindering the deal process, causing resentment among the investor base, and generally increasing costs.

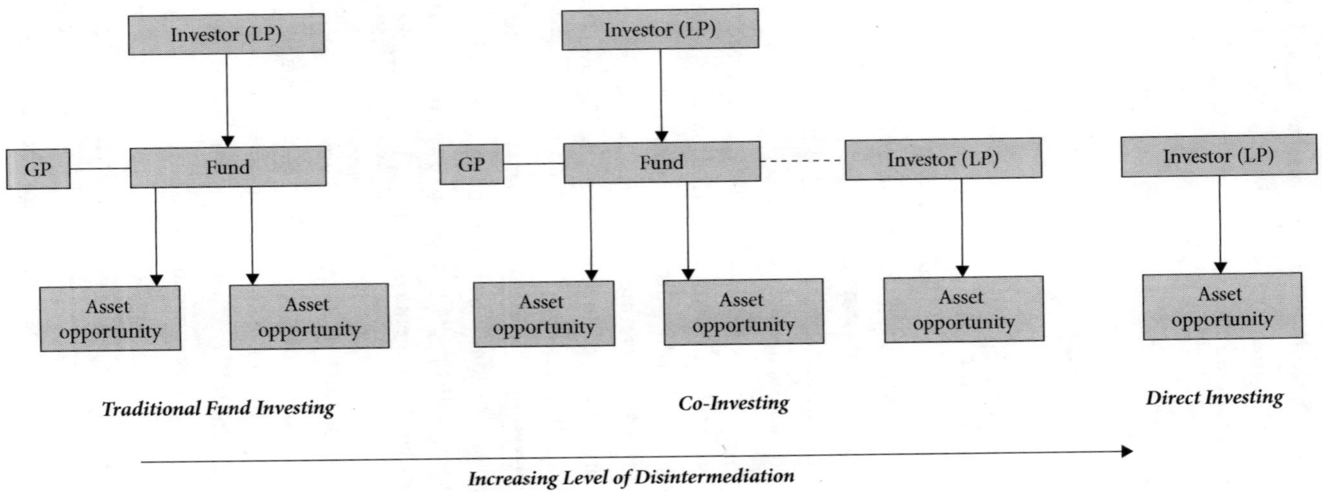

FIGURE 4.1 Different methods of private-market investing

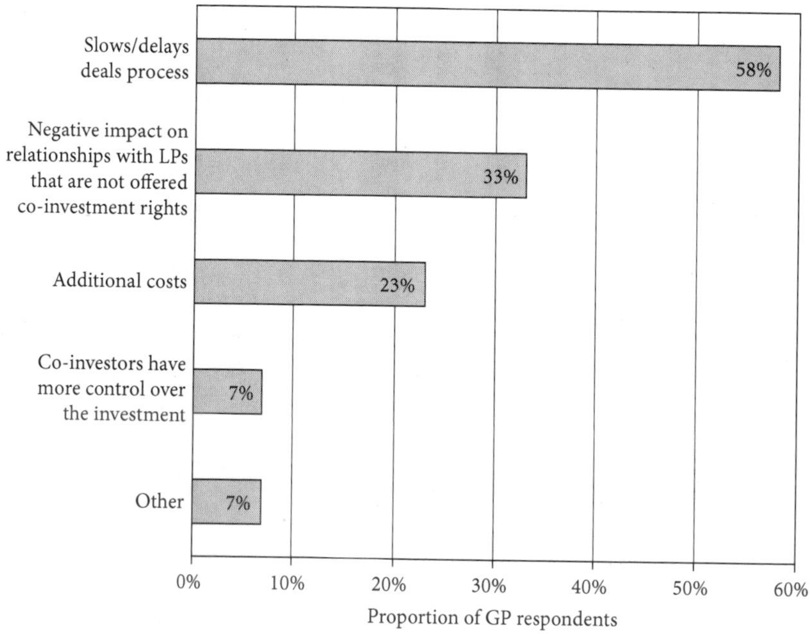

FIGURE 4.2 GPs' views on drawbacks of co-investments
SOURCE: Preqin 2014b.

While the co-investment option provides a step in the right direction for the fund manager offering, the mixed results indicate that there are limitations to this access point. An option for investors that has recently surfaced is to move toward the direct investing approach but to do so with the support mainly of peers rather than fund managers. The idea is to form collaborative vehicles that are independent of external fund managers and instead rely on the relationships and trust formed between partners. Such vehicles include the seed, joint venture, syndicate, and alliance and are illustrated in Figure 4.3.

Figure 4.3 shows the investor-led initiatives (seed, JV, syndicate, alliance) that form the collaborative or partnership-based model of institutional investment. These vehicles provide an alternative to the fund manager route and co-investment alongside the fund manager method.

Collaborative Investment Vehicles for Long-Term Investing

The collaborative investment vehicles outlined in Figure 4.3 are designed to use the social capital of investor organizations and formalize the close

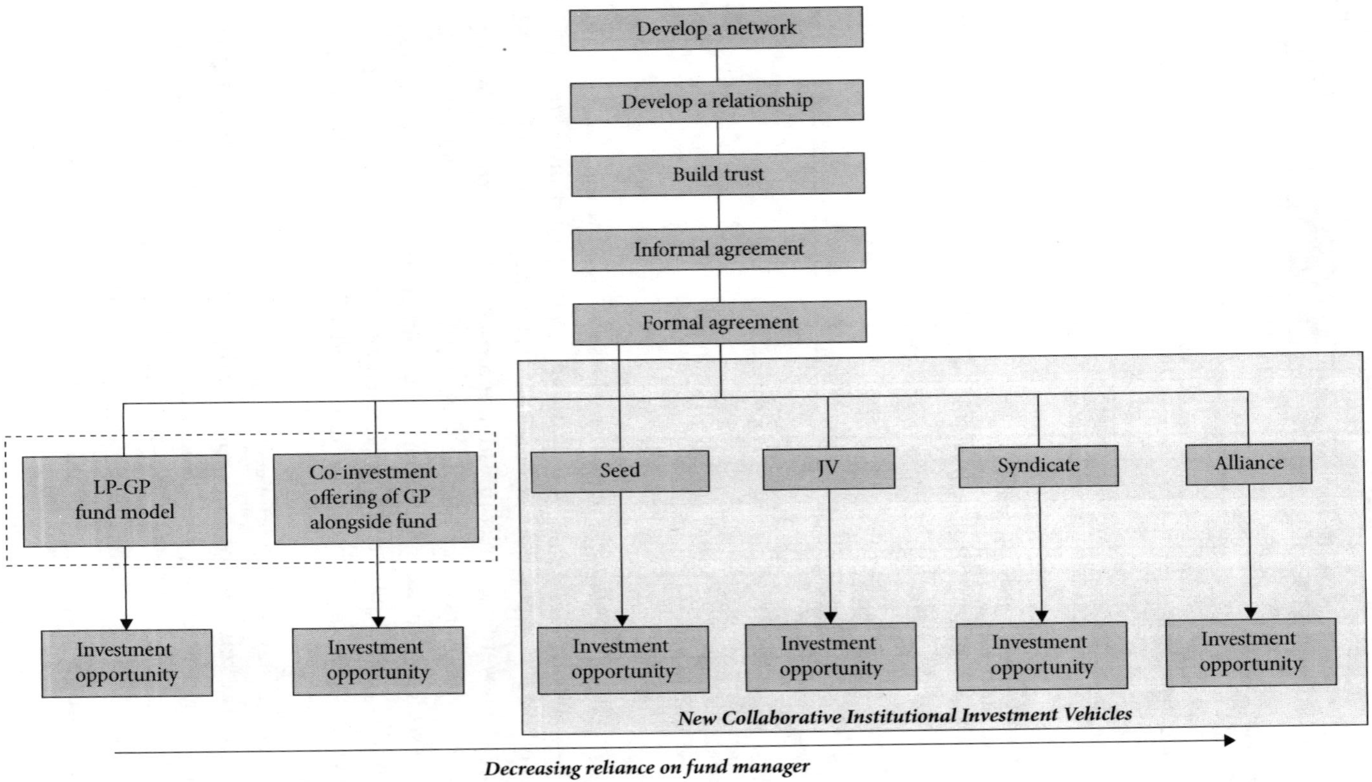

FIGURE 4.3 Collaborative investment vehicles for institutional investors

relationships that investors have with their investment partners into vehicles for efficiently deploying capital. Some of these will use fund managers in a discrete manner, while others will be completely independent and instead form partnerships exclusively with peer investors.

Bachher and Monk (2013) highlight the challenges and benefits of co-investment platforms using a case study of family office investors coming together to invest in clean-tech assets. From their interviews and case studies, they proposed the three types of investor-led co-investment vehicles: alliance, syndicate and seed. They outline what is involved, and the various considerations that need to be taken into account, when setting up each of these initiatives.

The *alliance* is a loose affiliation of like-minded investors coming together around a specific theme to share deals and resources. The objective is to somewhat formalize collaboration and co-investment, offering direct investors the opportunity to draw on a broader network without entering into legal agreements (e.g., seed) or dealing with the bureaucracy of external administration (e.g., syndicate).

The *syndicate*, on the other hand, is characterized by a more formal arrangement of like-minded investors around an investment theme to share deals and resources. Syndicate members make a formal agreement possibly through a credible and objective intermediary that will represent the affiliation externally, source and screen investment opportunities, and coordinate the sharing of information.

The *seed* has a formal legal structure (e.g., LLC) that brings together like-minded investors around a de novo asset manager staffed by a seasoned investment team. The objective of seeding a new asset manager is to maximize the alignment of interests between the asset owners and the asset managers by agreeing on concessions from the asset manager upon launch of the vehicle. A seeded vehicle is structured by the investors for the benefit of the investors.

A variation on the *seed* arrangement is that of using *platform companies* by institutional investors. *Platform companies* are generally independent companies operating in attractive investment niches. They are particularly common in emerging markets, and in acquiring and maintaining real assets, such as ports, dams, airports, timberland, energy, toll roads, and sometimes even specialized industrial companies. The idea is for the financial partner (asset owner) to take a meaningful position (ideally a control position) in a company and then use that company to make follow on investments or acquisitions in other assets within their specific niche or domain of expertise. The institutional investor helps roll up a variety of operating and development assets, while the company sources, screens, and invests in the assets while simultaneously managing them.

A variant on the platform company idea for institutional investors is that of a *joint venture.* Joint ventures have been prevalent in the corporate world for several decades as an alternative to acquisitions, contracting, and international development. Generally, a joint venture occurs when two or more firms pool a portion of their resources within a common legal organization.[5] Joint ventures are an increasingly common vehicle used by institutional investors to access certain private-market asset classes in geographies outside their own.

Academic literature has pointed to three general approaches for explaining the rationale for joint ventures. The first approach is derived from the theory of transaction costs as developed by Williamson (1985), who proposed that organizations choose how to transact based on minimizing the sum of production and transaction costs. Transaction costs refer to the expenses incurred for writing and enforcing contracts, for haggling over terms and contingent claims, and for administering a transaction. Joint ventures, by forming cooperative arrangements, can provide a solution for institutional investors to reduce the inefficiencies associated with economic transactions.

A second explanation for the use of joint ventures relates to how strategic behavior influences the competitive positioning of an organization.[6] In contrast to transaction-cost theory, strategic behavior is centered on how organizations can maximize profits by improving their competitive position. A strategic behavior perspective indicates that joint venture partners would be selected to improve the competitive positioning of the parties, whether through expansion or through depriving competitors of potentially valuable allies. Transaction-cost theory, on the other hand, posits that partners are selected to help minimize costs. While there are commonalities between the two approaches, both explain the motives to cooperate and select certain partners.

The third explanation is that organizations consist of a knowledge base, and joint ventures are thus a vehicle by which tacit knowledge is transferred.[7] The rationale is related to firms wanting to acquire the other's organizational know-how, or when a firm wishes to maintain an organizational capability while benefiting from another firm's current knowledge or cost advantage. In this case, where organizational knowledge is exchanged or imitated, such a process can itself be a cause of instability.

The theoretical rationale for joint ventures in the corporate world just described parallels the ideas of collaboration and innovation among long-term institutional investor organizations. Institutional investor joint ventures bring together a large source of investor capital with specific asset management or development experience in order to take advantage of important investment themes such as energy infrastructure, timber, and agriculture and earn high risk-adjusted rates of return. In this way, joint ventures can facilitate a long-term direct investment strategy of institutional investors.

The exact vehicle employed by investors for co-investing will depend on a number of factors including the specific characteristics of the organizations involved. The drivers for the adopted model are likely to be related to issues that need to be addressed for certain asset classes or geographies such as duration, alignment, sourcing, control, resources, knowledge, and diligence. Such a decision would also be affected by the internal capability of the individual investor driving the initiative forward.

These vehicles are intended to provide more alignment for investors and help them move along the spectrum to direct investing. Because not all investors have the resources and capability to lead a direct investment, these collaborative/partnership-based vehicles allow for investors with varying capabilities and provide a mechanism for achieving greater alignment for deploying capital. As a growing number of asset owners fear misalignment with traditional managers, it is no surprise that a variety of co-investment vehicles have emerged that pool institutional investor capital to invest in long-term assets in an efficient way.

Co-Investment Vehicles: Infrastructure Case Studies

The infrastructure asset class provides a useful example for illustrating the various benefits and challenges associated with setting up co-investment vehicles because of the large capital outlays required and the long time horizon of assets. The illiquid and opaque nature of infrastructure assets has made it challenging for institutional investors to invest directly into the asset class. In addition, various conflicts of interest have surfaced between investors and fund managers over fees and time horizon of funds. Therefore, a number of co-investment platforms have been set up to provide investors with a more aligned way of accessing the asset class, which theoretically should be ideally suited to long-term institutional investors. The framework for analyzing the case studies, including the implementation considerations for each of the vehicles, has been adapted from Bachher and Monk (2013). As will be evident, the networks of the investors in forming the vehicles were crucial. Thus, in Appendix 1 we include basic network figures of the main actors involved in the case studies showing how the investors came together to form the vehicles used to deploy capital into investment opportunities.

Industry Funds Management (Australia)

Drivers of the Initiative

Industry Funds Management (IFM) was formed over two decades ago. It is considered one of the pioneers of infrastructure investing and is often used as an example by other investor-led platforms because of its unique ownership structure.[8] IFM is an Australian-headquartered investment vehicle, owned by Australian institutional investors (superannuation funds), that now invests in infrastructure assets around the world. The Australian superannuation funds were formed as savings funds in the late 1980s. On the back of campaigns from the Australian Council of Trade Unions in 1992, compulsory super was introduced, requiring all employers to make mandatory contributions for their employees. The Australian superannuation system started with very small amounts in the 1980s, the biggest of which was around $100 million.

In 1990, the Development Australia Fund was created by Australian superannuation funds to pool together the different superannuation assets to aggregate their scale and invest in growing Australian private and public companies and infrastructure assets at low cost. In 1994, Industry Fund Services (IFS) assumed management of this fund with Development Australia Fund Management Limited as the trustee.

Structure

The structure of IFM has evolved since its inauguration in the 1990s, when 30 major not-for-profit pension funds pooled their capital together into a management vehicle, who then became the owners of the vehicle and are still the owners of the vehicle to this day. Initially, the management team consisted of just a handful of people, a secretary and a board, who were in charge of managing the investments. The IFS vehicle provided the formal platform to manage the pooling of the funds and deploy the capital into investment opportunities. At the early stages, the funds were advised by investment consultants who gave recommendations for most of the products invested into.

The initial founding documents of the initiative gave power to IFS (the management team) to nominate their own directors of the board, without any input from the pension fund owners of the initiative. The investment capability of the management team has evolved and grown over time. Initially the fund operated just as a fund of funds (investing in other funds such as Hastings and Macquarie for infrastructure), but as the team started to develop its capability and understand the market, they were able to do their own direct deals and ultimately now act as a fund manager for not only the initial founding superannuation funds but other institutional investors around the world. The process evolved from pooling assets to investing in funds, then being able to do co-investments, and then having the capacity to invest directly and manage their own assets.

IFM currently has AUD 31 billion in infrastructure assets split across global and Australian funds in open-ended structures. The IFM fund focuses on core, mature infrastructure assets in developed markets, primarily brownfield projects. The fund has an investment period that is ongoing and provides immediate exposure to income-generating assets (rather than a blind pool fund). IFM's fees are investor driven, not manager driven, and are therefore significantly lower than those charged by private-equity funds, meaning assets with appropriate risk profiles are selected and liability matching can be achieved.

Summary

The IFM model has been regarded as an exemplar for the establishment of collaborative infrastructure investment platforms. The investor ownership has enabled greater alignment for the vehicle, producing investment products

TABLE 4.1 Summary of IFM seed model

Size	AUD 31 billion (as of June 2016)
Strategy	Brownfield infrastructure OECD
Fees	0.5–0.6%
Structure	Open-ended

SOURCE: IFM 2016.

at low cost with returns going directly back to investors without significant dilution. IFM benefited from being an early mover in the infrastructure asset class, developing expertise in the area to be able to become a direct investor.

IFM has now evolved to become a fund manager raising capital from institutional investors from around the world.[9] As such, the original alignment of interests that underpinned IFM may not be as clear as they once were. Notwithstanding, they do remain a low-cost manager with deep experience in transacting and managing infrastructure assets.

One issue that IFM has had to address is the treatment of its founding investors as the company has grown in size. The model has had to evolve to keep up with the sophistication and growth of its core investor base. This issue of how to treat founding investors as the initiative grows larger and attracts capital from other investors has also occurred in other areas. For example, when endowments and foundations act as founding, cornerstone investors in

TABLE 4.2 Implementation considerations for IFM seed model

Vehicle type	*Seed*
Intermediation/administration	IFM management team
Enforcement	IFM acts as manager/intermediary and oversees all investment related activities
Mandate	Investment in core brownfield infrastructure in OECD countries
Membership	Thirty industry superannuation funds were the founders of IFM. Subsequently, IFM has become a fund manager raising capital from institutional investors around the world
Commitment	Investors are owners of the vehicle
Momentum	Size of assets steadily increases and allocation to infrastructure stays high at 12–13%
People	Expertise gradually increases over time through an evolutionary process, from consultants' advice to investing with managers to co-investments to doing direct investments
Competition	IFM has one of the largest AUM at AUD 31 billion and can therefore go after most deals they are interested in
Sharing	Not an issue as manager is owned by investors
Origins	The initiative was born out of the idea to pool superannuation fund assets together to achieve scale and invest on a lower-cost basis

SOURCE: IFM 2016.

alternative asset managers, their treatment when the managers grow in size and attract larger amounts of capital has made it difficult to maintain the close relationship that existed previously. The IFM model is based on a low-cost model, and the pooled product offering is still very much aligned for the large number of investors that are unable to invest directly.

Pensions Infrastructure Platform (United Kingdom)

Drivers of the Initiative

The Pensions Infrastructure Platform (PIP) was established as a collaborative effort between the National Association of Pension Funds (NAPF) and the Pension Protection Fund (PPF) to explore ways that pension funds could invest in U.K. infrastructure.[10] The PPF is a statutory fund run by a board, established under the provisions of the Pensions Act 2004.[11] The purpose of the PPF is to compensate members of eligible defined-benefit schemes in cases of employer insolvency where there are insufficient assets in the respective pension scheme. The NAPF is an organization set up to influence the outcome of and proactively shape U.K. pension policy; it comprises a board, an Investment Council, and a Retirement Policy Council.[12]

The NAPF and PPF have worked together since signing a memorandum of understanding (MOU) in 2011 to put forward a proposal that allows pension schemes to access the infrastructure investment market on more favorable terms than what were available through traditional fund managers. In September 2012, ten founding member pension funds came together to secure a critical mass for the initiative to move forward. Since that time, there have been monthly meetings among members to help develop the relationships and coordination of the group and alignment.

The founding pension funds contributed to the development costs of the fund and are linked in some way to infrastructure or technical industries.[13] The main issue that the investors voiced as a concern from their previous infrastructure investments was that the private-equity-style fee arrangements in most funds were too high and inappropriately structured for infrastructure investments, incentivizing managers to sell investments to realize their carried interest payments rather than to hold investments for the long term. The investors also had issues with the GP-LP relationship. LPs did not seem to be able to voice their concerns about the misalignment with GPs. It was felt that GPs were not representing LPs, and there seemed to be a significant governance gap. The key transaction that provided a lot of the impetus for investors to come together in the PIP was the Henderson infrastructure fund failure, where the acquisition of the John Laing construction firm resulted in considerable losses for the pension fund investors of the fund.[14]

Structure

The PIP top company is a not-for-profit entity owned by the NAPF and funded by ten pension funds making a commitment of £100,000 to cover development costs for the fund. The fund itself was to be structured as an English limited partnership model with the founding investors expected to make an initial investment of at least £100 million. Investments would also be taken from other pension plans. A management company (either third party or in-house) would identify, evaluate, and bid for potential investments and manage fund assets. An investment committee would advise the management company on bids and authorize major transactions. An advisory committee comprising LP representatives would monitor the success of bids and investments.

The original PIP structure is summarized in Figure 4.4. The Pension Infrastructure Fund originally had a target size of £2 billion and a target return

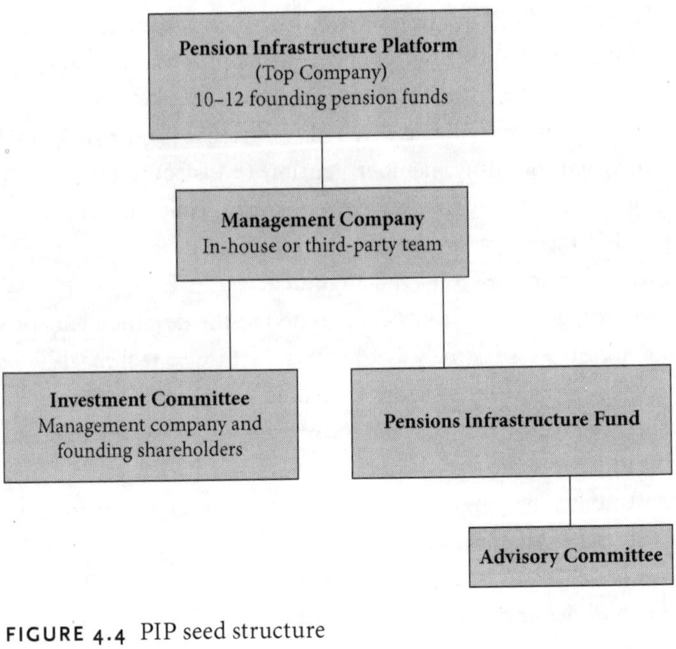

FIGURE 4.4 PIP seed structure
SOURCE: PIP 2016.

of Retail Prices Index (RPI) +2 to 5 percent. It was to be a 25-year closed-end fund with the ability to close after 10 years and after 15 years and the ability to go evergreen after 20 years. The fees for the managerial services of the PIP fund were targeted at 50 basis points, considerably lower than what is charged by traditional third-party managers.[15]

The fund's strategy was to invest in U.K.-focused assets that are inflation-linked in both equity and debt. There was a preference for smaller renewable-energy projects and social infrastructure such as schools and hospitals over large economic infrastructure. The fund would invest in less-risky brownfield assets initially and then gradually move into more risky investments.

Having a clear pipeline of projects in which to invest is crucial for an infrastructure fund vehicle. In the autumn 2012 statement, the U.K. government proposed more than £300 billion in infrastructure investments over the next 30 years, two thirds of which are planned to be private.[16] Because of the prominence of the PIP, it was initially envisaged that off-market deals would come

TABLE 4.3 Summary of PIP seed model

	Original fund structure (2012)	*1st fund launch (July 2014)*	*2nd fund launch (February 2015)*	*3rd fund launch (2016)*
Size of fund	£2 billion	£500 million	£250 million (target)	£1 billion (target)
Target return	RPI + 2–5%	—	—	RPI + 0–2% (debt) + 2–5% (equity)
Strategy	Low-risk, U.K. brownfield	Operational U.K. PPP assets	Solar, PV	UK infrastructure (housing), social infrastructure (hospitals, schools, flood defenses), communications, utilities (renewable), energy and transportation
Management	In-house	Third-party (Dalmore Capital Ltd.)	Third-party (Aviva Investors)	In-house
Time horizon	25-year, closed-end	—	—	—
Management fee	0.5%	Undisclosed	Undisclosed	Debt—0.35% during investment, 0.225% after investment Equity—0.5%, 0.45%

SOURCE: PIP 2016.

to the PIP; however, the sources of deal flow now would depend on the ability of the managers to attract deals.

Summary

The PIP fund can be seen as an example of the seed arrangement where a formal legal structure was used to collate investors together to invest into infrastructure assets. Relationships among the participating investors had somewhat already been established through their membership in the NAPF, which also provided the initial coordination and impetus for the initiative. The bond for collating together seemed to be the common understanding that infrastructure is an attractive investment area and that existing models for accessing infrastructure proved to be misaligned and ineffective. The role of the NAPF and PPF in formulating the idea of the initiative and then ensuring that a critical mass of investors was achieved was crucial.

However, while in theory the initial concept of populating an in-house manager to invest in infrastructure on more aligned terms provided an excellent solution to the issues faced by investors, a number of challenges have been encountered. First, it appears that knowledge and expertise in setting up the PIP has proven to be a key challenge. Finding the right talent to lead the operation of the fund and build a management team appears to have been particularly difficult: the CEO was not appointed until September 2014. This may be because the infrastructure investment market was an underdeveloped industry, making it more difficult to find the necessary skills without encountering conflicts of interest. As a result of the challenges in establishing an in-house manager, a third-party manager was instead chosen to run the initial fund. While the fee arrangements with the manager have not been disclosed, the negotiations were supposedly undertaken with the original principals in mind to offer "good value for money." The procedure for setting up the fund by starting with the investors was still new (in reverse) compared with how traditional infrastructure funds have been set up. While the preferred internal management team could not be formed initially, seeding a third party manager, as conducted here for the PIP, can be seen as a relatively aligned method for deploying capital in private assets.

The launch date for the PIP fund was originally scheduled for January 2013 but was then pushed back to the summer of 2013. An announcement for the selected manager was made over a year later in January 2014, with a target fund size of only £500 million, and the appointment of an internal CEO to build a larger fund was not announced until September 2014. The long time lag with the PIP fund illustrates the challenges associated with setting up such an initiative.

A large number of people were involved with establishing the PIP; this may have been a constraint, especially when trying to achieve a balance of power between the administrators, investors, and consultants.[17] This was the first time that a project of this nature had been conducted, and it is not clear whether governance and accountability were present at the outset. External consultants were engaged to advise on the shape of the PIP and the search for a management team, rather than PIP relying on the expertise within the investors' institutions; this may have introduced an additional layer of interests into the equation, thus reducing overall alignment of interests. An underlying principle of PIP was to create a new model, with investors wishing to distance themselves from traditional managers, whereas traditional managers and models formed the majority of past recommendations of consultants. The role of consultants and potential conflicts of interest that can exist have been documented.[18] If such conflicts of interest or lack of understanding existed, this could have contributed to the prolonged development process.

A lack of leadership could have resulted from an unclear governance structure at the outset of the initiative's formation. A benefit for future projects would be to have the governance of the fund established as early as possible to ensure that the setup of the fund could be carried out as efficiently and transparently as possible. If there is not full transparency over the decision-making process, the original aims may not be given precedence, resulting in confusion, damaged trust and relationships, and ultimately a less-than-optimum model. Installing a board structure made up of founding institutions and independent members might have facilitated the establishment of the fund and deployment of capital more quickly.

In the seed arrangement, there should be an emphasis on the intermediator/administrator role for the setup of the vehicle. During the setup of such a co-investment platform, the intermediator role requires personnel with significant experience in the field of institutional investment as well as a deep understanding of the underlying drivers for the setup of the platform.

Global Strategic Investment Alliance (Canada)

Drivers of the Initiative

The Global Strategic Investment Alliance (GSIA) is a global co-investment alliance platform launched in 2012 by the Ontario Municipal Employees

TABLE 4.4 Implementation considerations for PIP seed model

Vehicle type	*Seed*
Intermediation/ administration	During setup, administrative tasks were delegated to the NAPF; a third-party investment manager or internal team would then be the intermediator
Enforcement	Formal legal structure of fund polices the initiative
Mandate	Defined at inception; U.K. low-risk core infrastructure
Membership	Members primarily came from NAPF institutions
Commitment	Members contribute to the development costs of the vehicle as well as providing investor capital
Momentum	Momentum has been stalled because of ineffective leadership and various challenges have been encountered
People	The new CEO was formerly a CIO at a U.K. pension fund
Competition	Will be dependent on the structure of the final fund and the attributes of any third-party managers; the initial fund could be seen as one of the many in the market
Sharing	Not an issue given the legally binding structure of investors to the fund
Origins	The founding members of the PIP are bound by the common desire of wanting to invest into infrastructure assets in a more efficient and aligned manner

SOURCE: PIP 2016.

Retirement System (OMERS), a large Canadian public pension fund with net assets of CAN 77 billion (as of December 2015).[19] The GSIA was designed to gather sophisticated like-minded investors (mainly pension funds) to directly invest in infrastructure assets. Through the GSIA, participating alliance members invest in core infrastructure assets with an enterprise value of more than USD 2 billion in sectors such as airports, railways, ports, power generation and distribution, and gas pipelines mainly in North America and Europe.

The GSIA aimed to raise USD 20 billion, with OMERS providing USD 5 billion. In April 2012, Mitsubishi Corporation (MC) entered into binding commitments to jointly invest up to USD 2.5 billion in infrastructure assets, together with other Japanese pension funds and financial institutions, namely the Pension Fund Association, the Japan Bank for International Cooperation, and Mizuho Corporate Bank. In March 2014, OMERS entered into a co-investment agreement with Japan's Government Pension Investment Fund (GPIF), the world's largest pension fund, and the Development Bank of Japan (DBJ). This was followed shortly after by a commitment of USD 1.325 billion from a collection of U.S.-based Taft-Hartley "union" pension plans managed by U.S. manager McMorgan & Co. Participation by GPIF, DBJ, and McMorgan & Co. brought the total capital committed to the GSIA to USD 12.5 billion.[20]

Structure

All GSIA investments are originated and managed by OMERS. The investments made by the initial four Japanese investors are managed by wholly owned MC subsidiaries Double Bridge Infrastructure Inc. and DBI Management Inc. The investments made by GPIF and DBJ are managed by Nissay Asset Management and advised by Mercer; that is, opportunities presented by OMERS are screened and invested by Nissay Asset Management with Mercer advising Nissay. The operation and management structure of the GSIA is illustrated in Figure 4.5.

The GSIA charges a fee of 50 basis points on invested capital and a carried interest fee for performance at a later date, with OMERS managing the assets once they are acquired. A predetermined (negligible) payment is made by the investors to OMERS in order to cover sourcing costs. However, OMERS notes that the fee income is not the main attraction; rather the collaboration and size of investment power drives the appeal of this model (and its returns).

Summary

The GSIA can be categorized as a cross between an alliance and syndicate co-investment arrangement where one of the institutional investors takes on the lead role for sourcing and managing investments and effectively acts as the GP of the platform. The formality of the arrangement becomes realized once investments have been made.

The GSIA provides an example of how a large sophisticated investor can take on the lead role in a co-investment arrangement and help provide more alignment than the vehicles offered by traditional fund managers. Such an alignment enables other smaller institutional investors, without the ability to invest directly, to access infrastructure assets on more aligned terms and conditions than their default fund managers.

Once OMERS had conceived the idea of creating the GSIA, the organization then had to think about whom to partner with and the strategy for getting other investors on board. It would appear that the strategy employed by OMERS to find co-investment partners relied heavily on the relationships

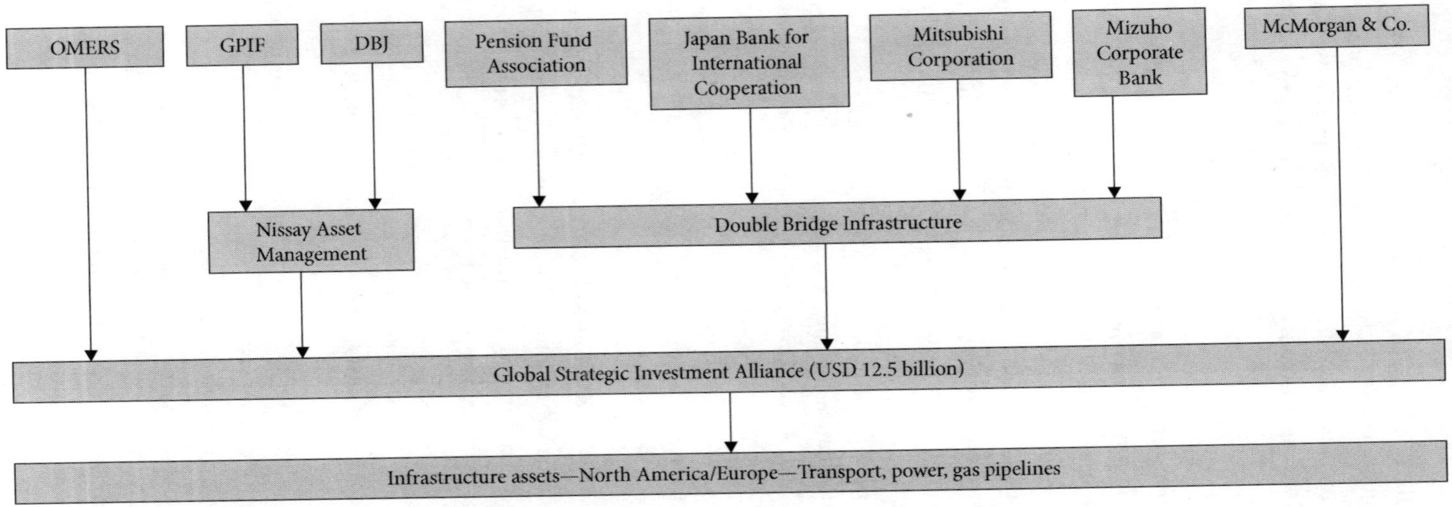

FIGURE 4.5 GSIA alliance/syndicate structure

SOURCE: Mitsubishi Corporation 2013, Jacobius 2014.

TABLE 4.5 Summary of GSIA alliance/syndicate model

Size	USD 20 billion target (OMERS USD 5 billion, total raised USD 12.5 billion)
Strategy	Brownfield infrastructure North America/Europe
Fees	0.5% on invested capital
Management	OMERS acts as lead investor and GP

SOURCE: Mitsubishi Corporation 2013, Jacobius 2014.

that the organization had with other investors (as opposed to a formal fund-raising process). OMERS, being a direct investor in private-market assets, had already developed a number of working relationships with other investors and were also members of the Long-Term Investors Club, which helped forge deeper relationships with their co-investment partners.

The fact that the Japanese co-investors had a significantly large capital base but little experience and yet an increasing appetite to invest larger proportions in alternative assets globally seemed to fit the objectives of the GSIA, where scale and reducing competition was a key driver for the initiative. The ability of the investors to leverage and learn from OMERS was also a factor in securing their partners' capital. Other more sophisticated, large investors, such as those closer to OMERS in Canada did not show the same interest in being part of the GSIA, primarily because the motivating factors were not as high as they were for the Japanese institutional investors; that is, the proposition of joining the GSIA for the large direct investors did not make much sense, as they would be able to achieve similar results on their own, without any other costs.

One issue that came up specific to OMERS leadership in the GSIA was the need for cohesion within the organization, particularly between the OMERS strategic investments division and Borealis, the infrastructure investment management division of the organization. Borealis is an experienced direct infrastructure investor and had already established a number of relationships with other investors through the transactions that they had previously completed. A challenge faced by the organization was to balance the expectations between the existing Borealis investor partners and the separate new co-investment partners in the GSIA. The well-developed silos in OMERS highlight the coordination issue between an individual department and the strategy of the entire organization. A key lesson here is that when developing a co-investment strategy at the organization level, there needs to be buy-in and a clear plan for how the strategy will be implemented across all areas of the organization.

Ultimately, the GSIA provides a good example of how a network of investors can facilitate the establishment of an aligned co-investment platform. As noted earlier, the benefit of collaborating not only allows for a better alignment of interests between investors but also enables a critical mass to be achieved so that the GSIA can access opportunities that previously were restricted mainly to large fund managers. The initiative formation has benefited from the extensive infrastructure investment experience of OMERS, although the silo nature of the organization emphasizes the need for greater firmwide collaboration. While the performance of investments is yet to be determined, the initiative has succeeded in achieving a number of its setup objectives.

TABLE 4.6 Implementation considerations for GSIA alliance/syndicate model

Vehicle type	*Alliance/syndicate*
Intermediation/ administration	OMERS (with sufficient expertise and sophistication) takes on responsibility for this role
Enforcement	The group police themselves; however, the opt-in nature of the investments reduce the need for this
Mandate	Investment in core brownfield infrastructure in North America and Europe
Membership	Investors with an appetite for this group of assets with a large capital base and long time horizon were targeted; organizations that had existing relationships with OMERS were approached
Commitment	Contribution to administrative costs and signing of the formal agreement into the alliance signal the commitment of the investors to the GSIA
Momentum	With so much capital raised into one vehicle, the potential size and power of the GSIA provides the momentum to deploy capital cooperatively
People	OMERS, as a pioneering institutional infrastructure investor, enables significant specialist expertise to be drawn upon for the GSIA
Competition	The size of capital raised in the GSIA enables the alliance to go after deals not possible for many other investors, thus reducing competition
Sharing	Sharing of information among GSIA members has been affected by existing relationships of OMERS with other investors
Origins	With the main lead of the GSIA being a long-term institutional investor, the common thread binding the investors together was evident from the start

SOURCE: Mitsubishi Corporation 2013, Jacobius 2014.

CPPIB Co-Sponsor Model—Buying into the 407 Express Toll Route

Drivers of the Initiative

The Canada Pension Plan Investment Board[21] (CPPIB) syndicate model provides a slightly more distinctive way of forming a co-investment partnership with other like-minded institutional investors.[22] After a partial acquisition of the 407 Express Toll Route (407 ETR) in Toronto, CPPIB then syndicated a portion of their stake in the asset to other institutional investors interested in investing in infrastructure.

CPPIB's strategy as a long-term investor would normally be to hold infrastructure assets over the long term. In this particular case of the 407 ETR, in order to gain access to larger and even more attractive opportunities, a "syndication at cost" model with like-minded investors was created.[23]

Structure

After closing on two separate transactions in late 2010 to acquire 40 percent of the 407 ETR for more than USD 3.5 billion, CPPIB was ready to syndicate up to 30 percent of this position. A confidential investment memorandum was sent to a select group of like-minded long-term investors, detailing key items about the transaction and the terms for syndication.[24]

Such a syndication requires a large institutional investor to take the lead and invest directly in an infrastructure asset. The lead then creates a vehicle to allow opt-in for additional investors, setting a minimum investment level. Each investor then does its own due diligence and decides whether to invest at the set price.

In the example of the 407 ETR, each investor needed to invest a minimum of USD 100 million and had 90 days within the investment closing date to invest. The management structure is subject to a vote each year so that the syndicate members can opt out if costs became too high or alternative options with fewer fees became available. There is no fiduciary obligation among members of the investor group. There are no ongoing management or performance fees, just a share of the acquisition costs and roll-forward at the expected IRR.

Summary

This CPPIB syndication of the 407 ETR is a slight variation of the syndicate model proposed earlier. The main difference is that there is no intermediary

TABLE 4.7 Summary of CPPIB syndicate model

Description	Up to 30% investment of CPPIB's stake in 407 ETR syndicated to other investors
Size	Minimum USD 100 million commitment. Syndicated 11% of 407 ETR
Strategy	Physical infrastructure assets, long-term cash flows, low risk profile, inflation protection
Governance	Investors nominate board seat—15% per nomination
Target return	IRR 11%
Costs	Share of investment and management costs on pro rata basis, subject to annual vote

SOURCE: Dyck and Virani 2012, Della Croce and Sharma 2014.

involved and instead of investing into a blind pool arrangement, the asset of interest is already identified.

The model here allows larger entities with in-house investment teams to invest in larger projects with lower competition, spreading risk among stakeholders. There are no extra fees for the lead investor, and each subsequent investor pays only the lead investor's pro rata costs.[25]

This type of model also allows smaller investors without in-house investment capability to invest into infrastructure assets with only a pro rata share of costs of the lead investor, much less than the fees from traditional fund structures. While the small investors must perform their own due diligence, the lead investor would have done the majority of the work.

A major issue for this model was the ability of the lead investor to attract other institutional investors to the co-investment arrangement. As was the case for the GSIA, the CPPIB syndication model was less appealing for other similarly large and sophisticated institutional investors compared with less-sophisticated investors looking to get exposure to infrastructure assets. The minimum investment required for the syndication was quite large and the deadline for the investment was quite tight, meaning that a certain size and decision-making capability was needed among potential investor partners. From CPPIB's perspective, the model is designed to take advantage of a large capital base and long-term horizon of institutional investors in order to access the assets in a more cost-effective way. The ability of the model to be replicated is questionable, given the lack of sizable infrastructure opportunities available in the market place.

TABLE 4.8 Implementation considerations for CPPIB syndicate model

Vehicle type	*Syndicate*
Intermediation/ administration	Provided by CPPIB
Enforcement	Not required, as investors will be governed by their investment contract
Mandate	Low-risk, long-term, inflation-protected infrastructure assets with equity value greater than USD 1.5 billion
Membership	CIM sent by CPPIB to other investors identified as likely partners
Commitment	Ensured by the investment contract based on the CIM
Momentum	Investors know what asset they are investing into and are driven by the partnership with CPPIB
People	The lead firm, CPPIB, is one of the most sophisticated institutional investors in the world
Competition	Not relevant given that the asset of interest is already known
Sharing	Official information disclosures regarding the investment will be made, and it is envisaged that the investor relationships will be deepened
Origins	A major reason for CPPIB to syndicate the investment is to help develop the relationships with other like-minded investors who could be partnered with on future deals also

SOURCE: Dyck and Virani 2012, Della Croce and Sharma 2014.

Ultimately, the syndication model could help overcome some of the barriers to private institutional infrastructure investment because of a greater alignment in terms of the investment horizon, investment philosophy, cost of capital, risk profile, and governance views.

Philippine Investment Alliance for Infrastructure Fund (Philippines)

Drivers of the Initiative

The Philippine Investment Alliance for Infrastructure (PINAI) fund is an unlisted fund dedicated to investing in core infrastructure assets in the Philippines. The fund concept arose from efforts by the government of the Philippines to find ways to catalyze private sector investment in infrastructure.[26]

Historically, institutional investors have predominantly focused on the supposedly less-risky developed economies of Europe, North America, and

Australia. The PINAI fund provides an example of how a fund can be set up with government involvement to help attract institutional investment in the much-needed investment areas of the emerging economies.

The fund was formed in reverse order compared with most other infrastructure funds, with the cornerstone investors first coming together before an appropriate manager for the fund was selected. Three cornerstone investors make up the fund: the Government Service Insurance System fund (USD 400 million), the Asian Development Bank (ADB, USD 25 million), and the Dutch pension fund asset manager APG (USD 150 million). After a thorough manager selection process, Macquarie Infrastructure and Real Assets (MIRA) was selected to manage the fund and will also provide equity into the fund (USD 50 million). The total size of the fund is USD 625 million.[27]

Structure

The fund is a closed-end fund with a time horizon of ten years. It is a combination of a Singapore-domiciled pooling vehicle Macquarie Infrastructure Holdings Philippines (MIHP), plus direct investors (ADB, GSIS, APG), operating together as a single fund pursuant to a co-investment agreement. PINAI is managed by MIRA, which is responsible for all major investment, divestment, and management decisions within the fund's overall mandate. An advisory committee (made up of the cornerstone investors) makes decisions with respect to expanding the fund's mandate and any related party transactions.[28]

Both the cornerstone investors and the manager were attracted to the idea of setting up the PINAI fund for a number of reasons: the Philippine economy has been growing strongly in recent years, including the move to investment-grade credit rating and continued strong GDP growth; the Philippines is home to one of the youngest and fastest-growing populations in Asia, which is likely to create a boom in working-age population over the near term, which in turn drives growth in demand for infrastructure; and the Aquino administration aimed to "invest massively in infrastructure" as one of the five key strategies outlined in its Philippine Development Plan 2011–2016, with a core component being to attract private investment in infrastructure.[29]

Summary

The PINAI fund can be seen as an example of the seed co-investment arrangement where the investors collate together around a certain theme (Philippines infrastructure) and then select a manager to manage the investments. In this case, Macquarie was selected as the manager for the PINAI fund but

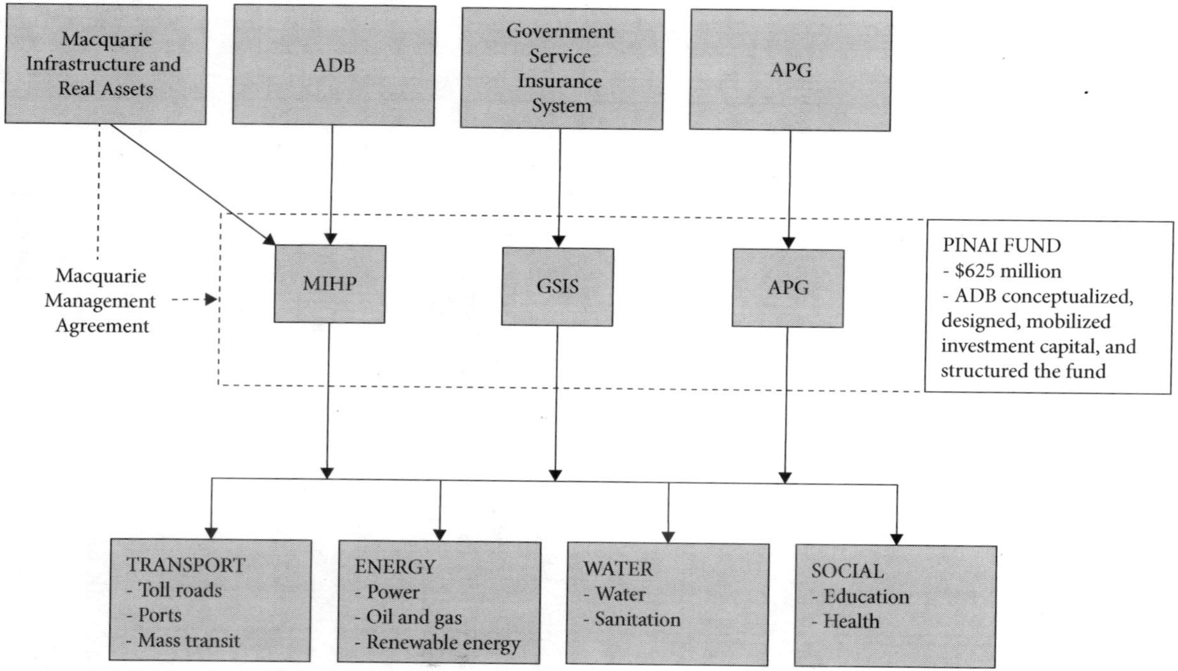

FIGURE 4.6 PINAI seed structure

SOURCE: Asian Development Bank 2016.

TABLE 4.9 Summary of PINAI seed model

Size	USD 625 million
Strategy	Brownfield and greenfield infrastructure in the Philippines
Fees	"Market" rate set by Macquarie (approx. 1.5%)
Management	Macquarie Infrastructure and Real Assets
Investors	ADB, GSIS, APG, Macquarie

SOURCE: Asian Development Bank 2016.

wouldn't be considered a de novo manager, given Macquarie's experience in setting up infrastructure investment funds. Macquarie was selected as the manager because of the organization's familiarity with the Philippines and with well-established securities and advisory businesses there, as well as its support services. The fund benefits from Macquarie's extensive experience in infrastructure investing and its strong history and track record of pioneering infrastructure investment in new markets.

The unique aspect of the PINAI fund was the close relationship between the manager and its investors because of the small number of parties. The investors in PINAI had a good understanding of market conditions and investment climate, which has made it easier to communicate with each other. While the investors have no formal role in management, mutual sharing of market information and insights greatly assists the sourcing, evaluation, and management of PINAI's investments.

In finalizing the time horizon of ten years for the fund, Macquarie argues that there needs to be a balance between the life of the fund and the long-term nature of the assets. Investors generally expect an opportunity to realize their investment after a defined period, with ten years considered a suitable period to implement management and business improvements.

While the performance results are yet to be determined, the PINAI fund is an example of how institutional investors can successfully select an experienced manager on slightly more favorable terms than what would be the case through a traditional fund manager structure. Despite Macquarie being a pioneer in the field of infrastructure investing, the organization has also come under scrutiny for its opaque, highly leveraged financial products with fees that do not always reflect the added value provided by the manager. By grouping together beforehand, the investors were in a better position to negotiate terms. The fact that Macquarie was investing a sizable amount of their own capital in the fund provided further certainty for the investors that their interests were aligned.

In replicating this model, one observation is that the investors would need to have a certain level of sophistication to carry out their manager selection, as well as have developed relationships with each other and prospective managers. At least one of the investors would need a good understanding of the experienced and best-performing managers in the investment area of interest. In this case, previous successful working relationships between ADB, APG, and Macquarie facilitated the manager selection. A common understanding of the rationale and objective for the initiative would also be needed among the investors, who individually may provide an element of expertise or competitive advantage, whether it be local knowledge, aligned investment philosophy, and so on. In the PINAI case, the inclusion of the government pension fund and Asian Development Bank indicates the importance of having public-sector influence for the highly political nature of infrastructure

TABLE 4.10 Implementation considerations for PINAI seed model

Vehicle type	*Seed*
Intermediation/ administration	Selected external manager—Macquarie (MIRA)
Enforcement	Governed by legally binding fund structure
Mandate	Invest in Philippines infrastructure
Membership	Investors comprising Government Pension Fund, Asian Development Bank and International Institutional Investor collated together initially to conceive the initiative
Commitment	This is shown through the investment contract
Momentum	Illustrated by the Philippine government's impetus for facilitating private investment in infrastructure
People	Significant expertise can be drawn on from Macquarie
Competition	With government backing, the ability to get access to deals will be enhanced; the fund is the biggest infra fund in the country
Sharing	By seeding a manager, the investors may have greater ability to develop a closer relationship with the manager and use this relationship for further organizational development and knowledge/deal sharing
Origins	The Aquino government's push for public private partnerships in the Philippines paved the way for interested investors to set up an appropriate vehicle for investing in the country

SOURCE: Asian Development Bank 2016.

investing. This may assist in sourcing deal flow, lobbying for favorable regulation and guarantees, and helping to satisfy the risk appetite of other potential investors.

Lessons Learned from Co-Investment Case Studies

The infrastructure asset class has emerged over the last decade as an attractive investment option for institutional investors looking to get access to long-term, stable, inflation-linked cash flows. In the early stages of the market, however, unlisted infrastructure financial products were structured like private equity funds with high fees and short time horizons despite infrastructure returns (and risks) being lower. As a result, spurred by a number of failures from the financial crisis, investors have been looking at alternative ways to deploy capital into the asset class. For this reason, the infrastructure asset class provides a suitable example to look at the effectiveness of investor-led co-investment platforms. Although several of the initiatives were at an early stage of their development, a number of lessons can be learned. For many of these vehicles, the setup phase is crucial for the subsequent success of the respective platform.

One key takeaway from the case studies was the importance of the intermediator or administrator of the vehicle. This is a crucial role to help bring the different members together and coordinate the different opinions and characteristics of investors. Insufficient expertise for this role may lead to a significant power asymmetry in the relationship, with intermediaries and the underlying mission of the group being overlooked. Such a power asymmetry may affect the trust that investor members have in the administrator and the initiative as a whole.[30] The administrator is essentially the leader, and along with strong leadership skills, investment experience is a crucial component to the leadership of such an investment vehicle. The issue of infrastructure investment experience was not encountered in the GSIA and CPPIB syndicate, where the leaders of both initiatives were experienced sophisticated direct investors in infrastructure akin to a fund manager, except more aligned with fellow long-term institutional investors. In the case of the PINAI fund, sufficient experience and knowledge of the sector was apparent among the initial investors for the fund in order to select their manager. Along with its sophistication as a new direct investor, the wide network of APG enabled it to form relationships with the ADB and GSIS, in a geography far from its home. The PINAI fund indicates how a close working relationship based on trust among the investors facilitates the intermediation of a co-investment vehicle and selection of an appropriate manager for the fund. The IFM model is unique in that it was formed at an early stage of development of the private infrastructure market, and the management team that was installed was able to progressively develop the necessary expertise to deploy investors' capital directly into infrastructure assets. Because they were early investors in the pioneering funds like Macquarie and Hastings, they achieved favorable terms and also were allowed to exit from these products as they developed their own expertise. Such an option might be difficult given the relative maturity that the market has reached.

Another consideration observed in the case studies was that when a larger investor was setting up a specific co-investment vehicle, they needed to ensure that the new vehicle did not disrupt existing relationships the investor had with other investment partners. The process for finding new co-investment partners must be approached in a way that does not adversely affect the perceptions and future relationships of existing investors. To avoid this, clear communication and transparency between silos within an organization and buy-in to the new strategy should be achieved across the organization as a whole. This may be difficult to accomplish with conflicting views surfacing between different sections of an organization. Strong leadership will be required to minimize any adverse effects in internal and external relationships. The case studies indicate that a collaborative environment within an investor organization may be a prerequisite for collaboration with outside organizations.

The case studies also illustrated how the mix of investors in a co-investment vehicle can be important. Variation in size, location, industry, and other characteristics enable different experiences to be brought to the table. This is particularly important in the highly political and sensitive infrastructure asset class and was evident in the PINAI fund. Having the government pension fund and development bank involved helped facilitate deal flow for the fund as well as provide confidence for other international investors to invest in the emerging Philippine economy. In the GSIA and CPPIB examples, the size and expertise of the lead investors meant that there was a significant gap and greater dependency on the leader. The case studies have highlighted the importance of having at least one member of the investor group with specialist expertise or a competitive advantage in the specific investment area of interest.

TABLE 4.11 Summary of key lessons from case studies

Governance	Needs to be clearly structured at the outset (particularly for the seed arrangement)
	Founding investors should be considered for the board
	Strong leadership and investment experience in management team/intermediation
	No conflicts of interest in the leadership team
In-house collaboration	Reduced silos within an investor organization/in-house collaboration is a proviso for external collaboration
Investor composition	Diversity in investor composition is important for accessing deal flow/regulatory issues in certain asset classes/geographies (e.g., infrastructure, emerging economy)
Trust	Close relationships based on trust should be formed by parties (investors, administrator/intermediator) prior to formally coming together

Perhaps the most important aspect observed in the investor-led co-investment vehicles was the need for trust between the investors and administrators of the fund. The setup of the initiatives was made a lot easier when relationships had been previously formed and a certain amount of trust had been developed between the parties involved. The co-investment vehicles were established as long-term partnerships as opposed to a short-term discrete contract. While many were governed by legal contracts, there was still a clear need for all parties to be bound by trust and transparency. A lack of trust caused many of the investor/fund manager relationships to break down, and so investors have had to work hard at building trust with their partners to ensure that their long-term relationships are successful. The networking relationships that were developed to form the vehicles are shown graphically in Appendix 1.

Table 4.11 summarizes some of the key lessons learned from the infrastructure co-investment case studies in this paper.

Platform Company and Joint Venture Case Studies

The platform company concept is a variation of the seed arrangement outlined earlier, in which an investor invests into a company that has specialist expertise in an area of interest. The structure of the platform may vary, but basically we define this vehicle as the situation where an investor invests directly into a development company or fund manager (essentially owning the company) and then provides investor capital so that the company can grow the business by making investments of its own. This provides a way for the investor to get access to specialist expertise in an attractive investment area in a more-aligned way because the investor determines the terms of the investment arrangement. The platform companies concept provides a means of getting closer to the direct method of investing. As with direct investing, however, certain challenges are associated with setting up these initiatives in order to reap the benefits.

As mentioned earlier, joint ventures are another form of vehicle that institutional investors have used to efficiently invest in private-market asset classes. Because of the large information asymmetries associated with private-market asset classes, institutional investors have trended toward establishing close relationships with experienced investors in certain geographies or development-type companies. Institutional investor joint ventures and platform companies bring together a large source of investor capital with specific asset management or development experience in order to take advantage of important investment themes such as energy infrastructure, timber, and agriculture and earn high risk-adjusted rates of return. In this way, joint ventures and platform companies facilitate a long-term direct investment strategy of institutional investors. The following case studies provide insights into how these vehicles can be set up, the considerations that need to be taken into account, and the benefits that can accrue back to the organization.

TIAA-CREF Agriculture Platform (United States)

Drivers of the Initiative

TIAA-CREF is a U.S.-based institutional investor managing $869 billion of retirement assets in the academic, research, medical and cultural fields since 1918.[31] The organization was one of the early institutional investors in global agriculture, having started in 2007. The investment thesis for agriculture centers on the increasing pressure on agricultural productivity due to global population increases, further industrialization placing a squeeze on agricultural land, and increased protein consumption placing an increasing demand on global grain. As this investment thesis was gaining traction, an early direct investment was made in a company (Westchester) that had deep experience and showed expertise in this niche area. Through this early portfolio investment in the space, TIAA-CREF were able to execute on their wider agriculture strategy, which has now grown to $8 billion of holdings.

Structure

The structure of the platform company evolved from a minority portfolio investment by TIAA-CREF in to Westchester (an agriculture asset manager invested in global agriculture assets), which was an initial investment to "test the waters" on the strategy and on the team. After three years of investing in Westchester, TIAA-CREF then acquired 80 percent of Westchester to take a controlling stake, leaving the existing management to own the remaining shares in the business. Westchester then became a subsidiary of TIAA-CREF. Following the acquisition of Westchester, TIAA-CREF subsequently created a limited liability company (LLC) to raise capital from third-party investors, which is then invested by Westchester. The structure of the LLC (as shown in Figure 4.7) was developed by TIAA-CREF to provide more alignment for TIAA-CREF's investment partners, who believed in the agriculture investment thesis without restrictions on time horizon and a fee structure that is commensurate with the long-term characteristics of agriculture assets. The investors as a group in the LLC get seats on the board and seats on the investment committee for investments made by Westchester. The initial size of the TIAA-CREF-led Global Agriculture LLC was $2 billion; it was launched in 2012 with the Swedish AP2, the Canadian bcIMC, and CDPQ as founding co-investors.

Summary

The TIAA-CREF agriculture platform company model is an example of how a large institutional investor came up with an innovative way to get access to an attractive long-term asset class more efficiently than via the traditional delegated fund manager route. The process for setting the vehicle up can be distinguished by two key steps (see Appendix 1 for an illustration). The first step involved identifying and getting comfortable with a very good external group that can get access to and invest well into the assets of interest. In order for TIAA-CREF to get comfortable with Westchester Group, they invested a minority amount from the TIAA-CREF general account. Through this initial investment, the investor determined whether Westchester had the right cultural fit, whether the right investment philosophy fit, and whether the people were the right types of people that TIAA-CREF wanted to bring on board.

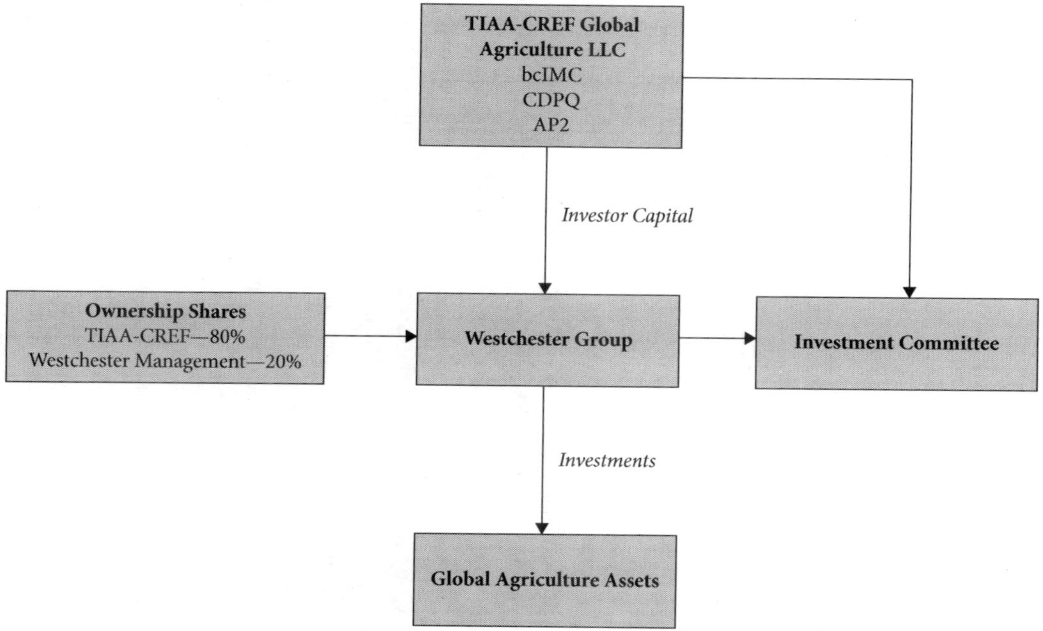

FIGURE 4.7 TIAA-CREF global agriculture platform structure
SOURCE: TIAA-CREF 2012.

TABLE 4.12 Summary of TIAA-CREF platform company model

Size	USD 2 billion
Strategy	Global agriculture (grain)
Fees	Undisclosed
Management	Westchester Group
Investors	TIAA-CREF, AP2, bcIMC, CDPQ

SOURCE: TIAA-CREF 2012.

The second step was the formation of the LLC to bring third-party investors on board. The initial period of getting other investors on board was similar to a typical fund-raising process whereby each investor did their own thorough due diligence. This was because the investors did not know each other and needed to get comfortable before committing to the partnership. However, once the commitment was made to partner together, their interests were aligned and the investors became not only friends but long-term investment partners. As a result, when similar platform companies were developed in other areas (TIAA-CREF also developed similar platforms for timber, oil and gas, and a second agriculture fund), the same investors from the initial platform company have also come on board, because the performance and trust have all been achieved from the previous initiative. The platform company initiative has enabled TIAA-CREF to develop deep relationships with its co-investors, who become the first port of call when they are trying something new.

In summary, the TIAA-CREF platform company vehicle is an example of the new collaborative/partnership-based model for long-term institutional investment based on close relationships between the management team and the investors in the vehicle. Agriculture investing as a "real alternative" asset class is less developed, is more illiquid, and has low correlation to traditional investments but has inflation-protection characteristics similar to commodities. It is thus theoretically ideally suited to the investment objectives of true long-term institutional investors. The platform company structure allows for more alignment between the co-investors in the vehicle and enables investors to get closer to the underlying assets of interest. The vehicle did require strong leadership from TIAA-CREF to drive the initiative forward.

TIAA-CREF needed the resource capability to make the initial direct investment into Westchester. TIAA-CREF is a hybrid type of investor that uses

TABLE 4.13 Implementation considerations for TIAA-CREF platform company model

Vehicle type	*Seed (platform company)*
Intermediation/ administration	TIAA-CREF/Westchester Group
Enforcement	Investors governed by terms of LLC structure
Mandate	Invest in agricultural land globally
Membership	TIAA-CREF lead investor, CDPQ, AP2, bcIMC (co-investors)
Commitment	This is shown through the investment contract in the LLC
Momentum	Primary drivers include increasing global demand for food, increased demand for protein diets, increased development squeezing agricultural resources
People	Significant expertise can be drawn on from Westchester Group, the entity through which investments are made
Competition	Selection of external management team is crucial in mitigating this risk; through an initial minority investment in the company, TIAA-CREF was confident that the investment objectives will be achieved
Sharing	By co-investing with peers, the investors have been able to develop deep relationships that have led to the group also investing in further platforms
Origins	TIAA-CREF's initial investment in Westchester Group in 2007 led to the formation of the wider platform in 2010

SOURCE: TIAA-CREF 2012.

both the direct method of investing (e.g., in infrastructure) and also indirect, delegated investing (in private equity). The platform company concept is also a hybrid type of vehicle that sits between these two methods. The strong leadership of TIAA-CREF has enabled other investors that do not quite have the same direct investing capabilities to get access to an attractive asset class in a more aligned fashion by partnering with peer investors in a more suitable structure compared to the traditional fund manager delegated investing method.

Cubico Sustainable Investments (Global)

Drivers of the Initiative

The Santander Asset and Capital Structuring division of the Spanish-based Santander Group began its operations in infrastructure finance by offering advisory services to the infrastructure sector in Spain in 2005 and started to make principal investments in energy projects in 2007.[32] Subsequently, the dedicated sustainable infrastructure investments team grew in size and reach to have a presence in other parts of Europe, North America, Australia, and Latin America. The team became a specialist in investing in renewable energy and water infrastructure with a strong track record investing in more than USD 2 billion of assets. The Ontario Teachers' Pension Plan and the Public Service Pension Plan (PSP) are both large sophisticated institutional investors with deep experience in infrastructure investing globally. The Cubico platform came about from the desire of large long-term investors to partner with an experienced management team to invest in long-term real assets without restrictions of time horizon and investment capital.

Structure

The Cubico platform was set up as a joint venture arrangement, equally owned by OTPP, PSP, and the parent group of the Santander Asset and Capital Structuring division infrastructure team. Cubico Sustainable Investments is a London-headquartered firm established to manage and invest in renewable energy and water infrastructure assets globally. The new company setup is led by the former Santander Asset and Capital Structuring team consisting of 30 investment professionals, and all 19 wind, solar, and water assets previously owned by Santander were transferred to the new company.

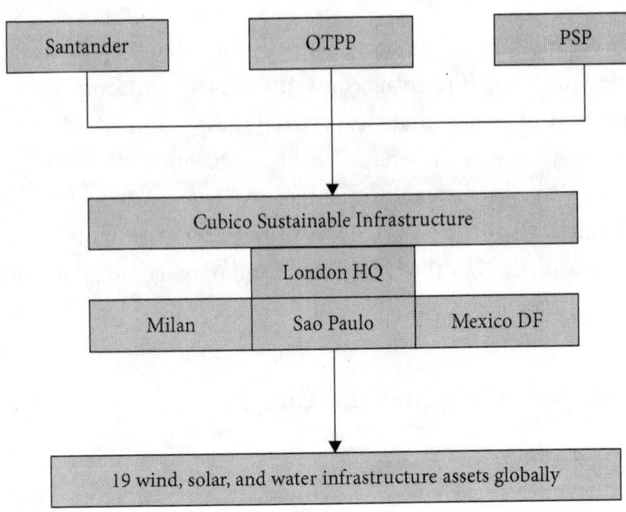

FIGURE 4.8 Cubico joint venture/platform structure
SOURCE: Cubico 2016.

TABLE 4.14 Summary of Cubico platform company/joint venture model

Size	Greater than USD 2 billion
Strategy	Sustainable infrastructure (energy, water)
Fees	Undisclosed
Management	Cubico (Santander)
Investors	OTPP, PSP, Santander

SOURCE: Cubico 2016.

Summary

The Cubico platform is a further example of how large institutional investors can invest in long-term real assets in a more-aligned fashion than traditional structures. In the Cubico example, the strong track record and expertise of the Santander Asset and Capital Structuring team was appealing to the two large institutional investors that were already large investors in the sustainable infrastructure sector. The proposition of partnering with dedicated long-term investors with few capital constraints for investing in further assets and growing the business was also very attractive to the Santander team. In such a vehicle, there are no constraints on the time horizon for investments, which in the sustainable infrastructure sector is crucial, because of the high capital requirements of the assets and long time lag before capital may be returned to investors.

Both institutional investors in this case are large sophisticated direct investors who have the resource capability to invest directly into infrastructure assets. Such expertise was required to be able to invest in the joint venture and perhaps also enabled the Santander management team to be comfortable not only that the investors were structurally aligned but also that they could contribute to future transactions in a slightly more meaningful way than a purely passive investor.

The key aspect here was that the large investors were able to leverage their competitive advantages of having size and duration to partner with a management team that has shown a certain amount of prowess and expertise (perhaps greater than their own) in an investment area of interest. In this sense, the investors had to develop their own sophistication in the investment area in order to get access to such a platform, which might make it harder/restrictive for other less-sophisticated investors to access a structure like Cubico. The

TABLE 4.15 Implementation considerations for Cubico platform company/joint venture model

Vehicle type	*Platform company/joint venture*
Intermediation/ administration	Santander
Enforcement	Investors governed by terms of joint venture structure
Mandate	Sustainable infrastructure investments
Membership	Santander, OTPP, PSP (co-owners)
Commitment	This is shown through the joint ownership of Cubico
Momentum	The global shift toward renewable sources of energy and water shortages globally
People	Significant expertise can be drawn upon primarily from Santander, as well as the joint owners (OTPP and PSP)
Competition	Selection of external management team is crucial in mitigating this risk; Santander has a proven track record in investing in over USD 2 billion in sustainable infrastructure
Sharing	The unique relationship allows knowledge sharing between the investors and the experienced, specialist management team

SOURCE: Cubico 2016.

attraction for the management team, however, was the ability to get access to a deep capital pool and not be restricted by time horizon for the investments.

CPPIB and Shapoorji Pallonji (India)

Drivers of the Initiative

CPPIB, as a globally diversified institutional investor, has been attracted by India as an investment destination for some time, and has had exposures to the country through general emerging market external managers.[33] One of the rationales behind increasing an allocation to the Indian market was the fact that India contributes close to 6 percent of global GDP. As a well-diversified global investor, CPPIB believes they should be working toward allocating capital to India in a way that reflects the country's contribution to global economic output. India is an economy that has risen to prominence over the last decade, partly because of the liberalization of foreign direct investment rules into the country and the critical need for real estate and infrastructure investments to help service the economic growth of the country. More specifically, the case for investment in India has been based on an advantageous demographic profile, a growing middle class, a healthy financial system, low levels of private and corporate leverage, and relatively conservative regulations. The economic liberalization and infrastructure investment trends have been further emphasized as high priority by the new prime minister, Narendra Modi, elected in 2014.

The Shapoorji Pallonji group is a large family conglomerate operating since 1865 with various activities including real estate development/construction, consumer products, business automation, and logistics.[34] Shapoorji Pallonji Co. & Ltd., specializing in construction, "design and build," and engineering procurement and construction (EPC), is the flagship company of the group. The mandate for the alliance was to acquire office buildings in the major metropolitan areas of India.

CPPIB has developed four key relationships with private Indian companies that represent collaborative types of investment partnerships: infrastructure development projects (through Larsen and Toubro, India's largest engineering and construction company); structured debt financing for residential projects (through Piramal Enterprises Ltd.); the third-largest private bank (Kotak Mahindra Bank); and in commercial real estate through the Shapoorji Pallonji Group.[35] While the relationships with Indian companies for investment were primarily originated by the CPPIB regional offices, such as the London-based real estate investments team, the organization used the services of an Indian-based consultant, Vikram Gandhi, who provided crucial background checks and confirmed reputations. Gandhi, a native of India but with extensive investment banking experience out of New York, was brought on as a senior advisor to CPPIB for its investments in India. Since March 2012 Gandhi has been on the ground in India to support the CPPIB regional office teams for evaluating potential partners to invest with. Shapoorji Pallonji is one of these partners.

Structure

The joint venture arrangement was announced on November 28, 2013, as a strategic alliance between CPPIB and Shapoorji Pallonji (SP) to invest in office buildings leased to prominent tenants in the major metropolitan areas of India, with scope for value-add returns from active asset management. CPPIB owns 80 percent of the venture, named SPREP Pte Ltd., with an initial equity commitment of USD 200 million. Both parties shared the development costs as per the 80/20 joint venture arrangement. The board of the entity consists of five members, three from CPPIB and two from SP. The investment committee has three members, two from CPPIB and one from SP. A fee structure is paid by CPPIB to SP; it is a combination of management fee, acquisition fee, and performance fee. These fees are significantly lower than what would be charged by a fund manager in a typical GP-LP blind pooled unlisted fund.

The joint ventures that CPPIB have set up in India, including the SPREP Pte Ltd. venture, are not intended to be evergreen in nature. The arrangement was set up for an initial two-year period with the option at that point to extend based on how effectively the partnership was working. While the decision to continue would be agreed on by both parties, this would be based on

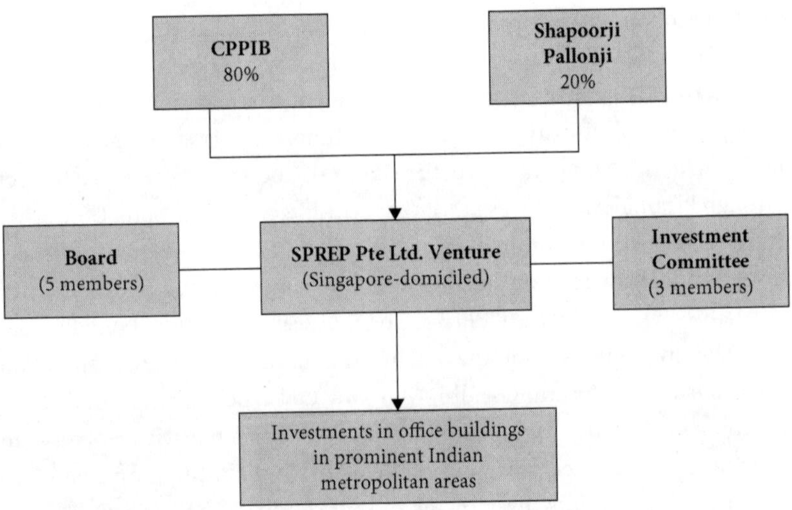

FIGURE 4.9 CPPIB/SP joint venture structure
SOURCE: Sarkar 2013.

TABLE 4.16 Summary of CPPIB/SP joint venture model

Size	USD 250 million
Strategy	Commercial real estate, Indian cities
Fees	Management, acquisition, performance
Management	Shapoorji Pallonji
Investors	CPPIB, Shapoorji Pallonji

SOURCE: Sarkar 2013.

the effectiveness of closing deals and the quality of the deal pipeline brought forward by SP.

CPPIB looks to partner with entities that have a long-term focus and can put their own money to work in the ventures as well. While there are no exclusive tie-ups, the pension fund prefers to maintain partners with whom they have a good relationship.

Summary

CPPIB has developed a reputation as one of the most forward-thinking and sophisticated long-term institutional investors in the world. As a large fund, they were one of the first to employ the direct method of investing by adopting a governance structure and building internal resources to originate, structure, acquire, and manage long-term private-market assets without having to rely on external managers for these services. These same internal resources enabled the firm to actively think about having a meaningful investing presence in India, an attractive emerging market, but with various challenges and difficulties for deploying capital.

Having established the internal view on investment in India, the subsequent question for the firm was which vehicle to use to make the investments. Direct investing in developed markets can be a difficult proposition, let alone in an emerging economy, which may have very attractive investment characteristics but in which the foreign investor does not have much local knowledge or experience.

Because Indian private markets are an attractive investment area, but one with many information asymmetries, the need to form relationships with experienced and trusted partners to invest in such markets was even more essential. As a sophisticated, direct investor, CPPIB determined that getting access to attractive investment opportunities in the most efficient way possible was a key objective. The platform company or joint venture vehicle seemed to be very appropriate for them. In order to find the right partner to invest through, CPPIB used an advisor to help the firm deepen their understanding of the investment environment as well as understand who might be the best to form partnerships with. The Shapoorji Pallonji joint venture was established in this way with the process progressively moving from the regional office investment teams scanning the market with the aid of an advisor to actively partnering with a local, on-the-ground expert with a long track record in a vehicle that provides long-term alignment and the ability to free up capital

TABLE 4.17 Implementation considerations for CPPIB/SP joint venture model

Vehicle type	*Joint venture*
Intermediation/ administration	Shapoorji Pallonji
Enforcement	Investors governed by terms of joint venture structure
Mandate	Invest in office buildings in metropolitan areas
Membership	CPPIB, Shapoorji Pallonji
Commitment	This is shown through the joint ownership of SPREP Pte Ltd.
Momentum	Micro- and macroeconomic growth prospects
People	Significant local expertise can be drawn upon from Shapoorji Pallonji; CPPIB is a sophisticated global investor whose experience will be invaluable for the venture
Competition	Both parties to the initiative have demonstrated track records in investing and in real estate development respectively and are in a good position to leverage their experience to execute on the mandate
Sharing	Shapoorji Pallonji will benefit from the relationship with a sophisticated long-term investor that has a large amount of capital and long duration; the venture will enable CPPIB to further develop their relationship with an experienced Indian-based development/investment firm and in the process learn more about the dynamics of investing in India
Origins	CPPIB consultant given mandate to find investment partners; SP selected from a shortlist of three

SOURCE: Sarkar 2013.

as needed. The process of finding a partner such as SP took approximately eighteen months.

Just as in the previous case studies, the vehicle is structured in a way that allows the institutional investor to leverage off the expertise of the local expert, while the development partner in the joint venture is able to get access to unconstrained long-term capital and partner with a sophisticated long-term investor.

Caisse des Dépôts International Co-Investment Joint Ventures (France)

Drivers of the Initiative

The Caisse des Dépôts Group (CDC) is a long-term investor based in France with the mission to support public interest and economic development.[36] The CDC group was established in 1816 to restore confidence following the financial crisis after the Napoleonic Wars and currently has a total asset base of approximately €400 billion.

As part of its international investment and development objectives, CDC was a founding member of the Long-Term Investors Club and the Institutional Investors Roundtable (IIR). In November 2013, by the directive of CEO Jean-Pierre Jouyet, CDC International Capital was established as a subsidiary of the group dedicated to building investment partnerships with sovereign funds and other international institutional investors. The impetus for setting up CDC International Capital had come about as a strategic priority to catch up with other major economies such as the United Kingdom, who had been more successful in attracting foreign capital into their economy. There was a desire for CDC to be more operational and business oriented. Therefore, 20 people were brought on board to establish CDC International Capital, 14 of whom were investment professionals and 6 were back-office staff. Three members of the team are responsible for each of the separate relationships formed.

In effect, CDC International Capital was set up to operate joint ventures with investors it had formulated close relationships with at the IIR, in particular Qatar Holding, Abu Dhabi–based Mubadala Development Company, and the Russian Direct Investment Fund (RDIF).[37]

Structure

Each of the joint ventures took three to four years of meetings to build the trust required to become partners. Signing a memorandum of understanding (MOU) was an important step to formalize the meeting conversations into a tangible arrangement. Signing a formal legal joint venture structure between the two parties enabled resources to be deployed to the initiative.

Each of CDC's joint ventures has different objectives. The arrangement with Qatar Holding is a 50/50 joint venture that invests 100 percent in France in various sectors. The relationship with Mubadala is formally two structures for tax purposes and has a mandate to invest in France but also in other geographies of interest where there may be strategic and competitive advantages. The agreement with the Russian Development Investment Fund was structured more like a private-equity-type fund, registered in the Netherlands, and possibly open to other investors in the future. The objectives of this fund were linked to the bilateral development of the countries involved and, specifically from the Russians' perspective, to help build more trust with the West.

TABLE 4.18 Summary of CDC co-investment joint venture model

Size	€300 million × 3 joint ventures
Strategy	Private equity, infrastructure, real estate
Fees	Share of investment costs
Management	Jointly managed
Investors	CDC-Mubadala, CDC-RDIF, CDC-QIA

SOURCE: CDC International Capital 2016.

Each partner in the joint venture has committed €150 million, with CDC initially allocating €450 million to the initiatives. Each of the relationships will develop more refined mandates, but initially there is an open-minded and flexible approach to the sourcing of deals from the networks of those involved.

Summary

CDC International Capital provides an interesting example of a long-term institutional investor that has recognized the benefits of partnering with other peer investors to achieve its objectives. Both Qatar Investment Authority (QIA) and Mubadala see the benefit of partnering with a direct investor that may have proprietary deal flow and access in France and Europe, while CDC are able to align themselves with like-minded peers for their investments. The RDIF joint venture similarly allows proprietary investments to be made in Russia and France in a reciprocal fashion. A fundamental requirement before putting pen to paper in drawing up these co-investment arrangements was developing enough trust among the participants of the initiative. The development of trust can be a lengthy process but well facilitated by investing time and resources in building an efficient network. This was clearly evident in the case of CDC, whose partnerships stemmed from the trust relationships that were developed through involvement at the IIR.

The CDC co-investment partnerships exemplify the collaborative model of investing. Their network- and trust-building exercise was facilitated through their involvement in the IIR, which enabled them to meet with partners (weak ties) that they otherwise might not have connected with. Joint ventures were used to formalize the initial relationships developed, and the organizations are now in a position to jointly deploy capital into private assets. While the

TABLE 4.19 Implementation considerations for CDC co-investment joint venture model

Vehicle type	*Co-investment joint venture*
Intermediation/ administration	Shared
Enforcement	Governed by joint venture agreement
Mandate	Invest in specific countries of interest (private equity, real estate, infrastructure)
Membership	Sovereign wealth funds in France, Abu Dhabi, Qatar, and Russia
Commitment	This is shown through the joint venture agreement
Momentum	Support of governments for investment geographies
People	Significant expertise can be drawn on from sophisticated direct investors
Competition	With government backing, the ability to get access to deals will be enhanced
Sharing	Each member will have access to attractive investment opportunities in their partners' jurisdiction
Origins	The mandate given to CDC International Capital to develop co-investment joint ventures was the driving force to help establish the IIR and subsequently form aligned partnerships

SOURCE: CDC International Capital 2016.

CDC partnerships are arguably politically motivated to help attract capital into certain jurisdictions, the case here shows how new efficient vehicles independent of managers are being structured to help facilitate the flow of long-term capital into private-market assets.

Summary

A growing number of investment vehicles can be characterized as investment collaboratives pooling and deploying long-term investor capital in creative ways. These vehicles are premised on asset owner organizations allocating capital to long-term private-market assets such as infrastructure, private equity, energy, agriculture, real estate, and timber. The vehicles are all distinguished by the innovative structures that are used to help investors get more direct and efficient access to the underlying assets of interest than what would be the case when using external managers in the traditional fund model. These vehicles are driven by the asset owners themselves in order to achieve more alignment when deploying capital in these assets.

The types of vehicles that have been outlined in this chapter are summarized in Figure 4.10. The examples in Figure 4.10 are not meant to be exclusive but provide the reader with the general characteristics that we believe are common for these types of vehicles. These vehicles are differentiated because they are usually formed independent of a fund manager unless the management team has been seeded by the institutional investor organization themselves. This is not to say that alignment cannot be achieved by using external managers (as discussed in Chapter 3); however, certain investors prefer to invest with their peers or with specially selected partners who share the same long-term objectives and alignment for their investments. We have collated a partial database of the current collaborative vehicles that have been set up. These are shown in Appendix 2. Interestingly, over half of the collaborative vehicles have been set up since 2014.

The types of investors employing the collaborative or partnership-based model of institutional investment seem to be at the more sophisticated end of the spectrum of long-term investing with direct investing capabilities. Direct investing capabilities may be required in order to set up these initiatives, which may restrict a large portion of the investor universe from partaking. However, in some of the co-investment platforms and platform company cases, the initial lead investor has sought to raise third-party capital, providing opportunities for smaller, less-sophisticated investors to also invest in these assets in a more-aligned way. Some of these vehicles have a minimum investment amount that may preclude certain investors. The formation of low-cost entities that help pull assets together in order to get above the minimum investment amount was seen in the GSIA and CPPIB syndicate models. Crucially, the net returns after all costs would need to be considered to determine whether such an investment meets an investor's long-term investment requirements.

In order to make all this work, institutional investors must develop their network to form trusted relationships with investment partners. In some cases, the existing network of investors drove an initiative forward. In other cases, the lead investors used resources to develop and strengthen relationships with certain individuals or entities with the hope that the relationships would eventuate into the signing of a formal memorandum of understanding and aligned capital deployment arrangement. The development of these relationships for the vehicles is shown graphically in Appendix 1. The networking exercise was needed on both the buy side and sell side of the transactions

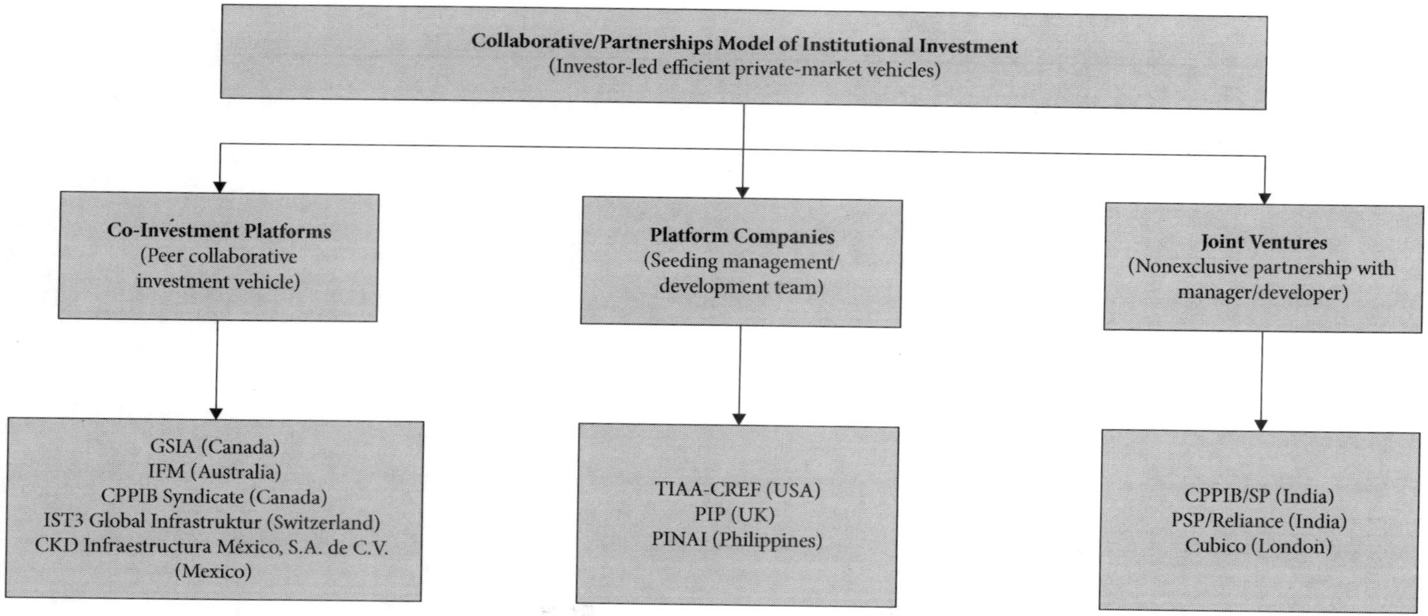

FIGURE 4.10 Examples that define the collaborative/partnership-based investment vehicles

of interest given the large information asymmetries associated with private-market investing. By developing their network, asset owner organizations are more likely to form relationships with potential investment partners and are more likely to know about the best opportunities suited to them as well as the most efficient and aligned way of accessing them. In this way, the collaborative model of institutional investment cases outlined in this chapter illustrates how the different components of re-intermediation are currently being executed.

As the concept of re-intermediation becomes more widespread and the collaborative model is increasingly adopted, traditional financial intermediary firms will need to rethink their own business models and determine how their expertise and service can best fit in with the new trends occurring in the industry.

5 The Future of Long-Term Institutional Investment

INSTITUTIONAL INVESTOR ORGANIZATIONS are facing a variety of intractable and hard to overcome long-term investment challenges. In the face of these hurdles, we hope this book offers some scope for optimism and even solutions. We believe collaboration and cooperation among peers is a way for long-term investors to take advantage of their idiosyncrasies to build capabilities and make investments in more aligned and efficient ways, especially when compared with the traditional fund manager route. Central to this concept is the need for investor organizations to systematically develop an efficient and effective network, enhance their social capital, and facilitate co-investment partnerships. An effective investor network is not limited to the relationships developed with other peer investors, as there is a wide range of organizations, individuals, contacts, and services that can help long-term institutional investors source opportunities with attractive rates of return. Re-intermediation, which is the central tenet of this book, is about investors approaching all relationships, with peers, fund managers, and stakeholders of all kinds, in new ways. Specifically in the case of managers, re-intermediation means rebalancing the power asymmetry that has too often favored managers and weighting it back to more appropriately represent investors' and beneficiaries' interests.

Significant information asymmetries are associated with investing in private markets. In this regard, intermediaries played a justifiably important role in the process. But the role of these intermediaries has evolved from that of a catalyst to one that is better described as a toll collector. For the future of long-term investing in private markets, and as part of the re-intermediation process, the business models of financial intermediaries, such as asset managers, consultants, and placement agents, need to be redefined. Their relationships with investors need to go beyond formal contracts and instead be forged on a long-term cooperative partnership underpinned by transparency and trust. Re-intermediation is thus all about fostering a new generation of aligned intermediaries that can help re-root institutional investor capital into the real economy.

Therefore, this new generation of intermediaries is required to support the professionalization movement in asset owner organizations. The collaborative, cooperative, and relational strategies of investors, outlined in this book, are part of the innovative ways institutional investors can overcome some of the challenges associated with this shift away from a reliance on traditional financial intermediary services.

As a result of this shift, investors in the future will rely on network economies instead of the agglomeration economies that they previously had access to through their intermediaries.[1] Financial centers such as London, New York, Hong Kong, and Sydney, where many financial intermediaries are headquartered, produce a range of agglomeration economies in addition to offering a wide range of complementary services that long-term institutional investors located in financial outposts cannot replicate.[2] Investors need to forge new relationships with intermediaries but also develop networks that help supplant the role that has traditionally been played by intermediaries.

In our view, this begins with institutional investors deepening their collaboration with one another. It also extends into a whole host of new kinds of relationships with managers, service providers, and consultants. After all, if you're going to move away from the existing set of intermediaries and all the economies of scale they enjoy, then you're going to have to replace them with something else. In our humble opinion, the collaborative model of investing offers a pathway to filling this void and will thus deeply impact and shape the institutional investment management industry in the future.

The Collaborative Model—Implications for Investors

The collaborative model of investment is premised on relationships with trusted investment partners. The objective is to deploy capital into private-market assets in the most efficient way possible. To date, sophisticated institutional investors have led the way in setting up the vehicles that characterize the collaborative model, indicating that a certain level of governance and resource capability is required to affiliate with peers and service providers on coherent and consistent terms. An investor's collaboration strategy is often dependent on its own characteristics. For example, our research shows that investors in the "Very Large" and "Mega" categories (defined by the WEF as having AUM greater than $25 billion) are most likely to initiate collaborative investment vehicles or joint ventures, co-investment platforms, and platform companies. The desired network and process for building such a network would thus be different from those that would be categorized as medium or large investors with AUM of less than $25 billion.

Whatever the size and scope of the investor, collaboration provides plentiful mutual benefits. Smaller "Medium" and "Large" investors would benefit from interacting with "Very Large" and "Mega" investors in order to learn best practices and other functions that these investors carry out. The smaller investors would also benefit from opportunities that may come about from their larger peers setting up co-investment platforms or other aligned vehicles in special opportunities. From "Very Large" or "Mega" investors' perspective, it would also be beneficial to develop relationships with their smaller peers in order to help them raise capital into the vehicles that they have set up or collect local knowledge in a small investor's home jurisdiction. "Very Large" and "Mega" investors would need to ensure that the investors that they bring in to their initiatives would have a requisite level of sophistication and governance capability to fulfill their obligations as a co-investment partner.

In terms of accessing opportunities, "Very Large" and "Mega" categories of funds would be looking to find specific development companies or management teams that they can directly invest in or form joint ventures with. This may come from their existing exposure with certain funds or partners on existing deals where a certain amount of trust and performance has already been established. In new asset classes or geographies, employing a local consultant to scope the opportunities and market may be required before formally committing to investment partners. For "Medium" and "Large" funds, opportunities may come directly from managers that already have existing mandates. The difference here is to re-intermediate with these managers to form separate managed accounts and an IMA that outlines how both parties can jointly examine opportunities and share the spoils.

While this re-intermediation offers many benefits, there are also challenges. For example, investors generally compete for deals and the best investment opportunities, so why would investors would want to bring their competitors into the deals that they have sourced? Certain deals in the private markets are sufficiently large that they require amounts of capital beyond the scope of one investor, but this isn't necessarily a universal truth. Co-investing with peers allows certain investors to achieve necessary scale in a more-aligned way and also helps large investors reduce their risk concentration in any particular asset. This was particularly evident in the co-investment platforms that have been created for the infrastructure asset class. Having a diverse investor base also brings differing viewpoints and expertise to the table with the investments. By building trust with respected partners, a family of peer investors can be created that can be the first port of call for future investments, as has been the case for TIAA-CREF with its investment partners in its initial agriculture platform. The key aspect in co-investment arrangements is for the parties to understand the respective competitive advantages and what each party might bring to the table in a collaborative endeavor (over and above just an outlay of capital).

With regards to the question of competition versus collaboration, Powell's (1998) research on collaboration among biotech firms seems applicable to LTI collaborations: "Since a competitor on one project may become a partner on another, the playing field resembles less a horse race and more a rugby match, in which players frequently change their uniforms." He also notices from his study on the biotechnology industry that heterogeneity and interdependence are greater spurs to collective action than homogeneity and discipline, which is a prime motivator for collaboration among heterogeneous institutional investors.

While the collaboration strategy we talk about here is about organizations pooling together, the personal relationships between individuals will determine the success or failure of the overall organizational objectives. Research indicates that strong relationships and mutual acquaintances tend to develop between people with similar social attributes such as education, income, occupation, and age. The operational guide to the formation of close, trusting relations seems to be that "a person more like me is less likely to betray me." Such relationships take time and resources to develop. The roundtables and research clubs outlined in Chapter 2 can help build trust in these relationships among LTIs. Intermediaries, on the other hand, have recognized the importance of the relationship-building process and devoted significant budgets toward it. While investors do not need to go to the elaborate and at times excessive lengths that intermediaries go to, they should at least recognize that if done properly, investing time and resources into relationships can add value to the organization in the long run.

In sum, a collaborative strategy can provide many benefits, and this book has sought to provide guidance on how an investor can incorporate a collaboration strategy into their organization. Tools will be needed to facilitate this. While a basic CRM software tool may suffice in the beginning, a modeling tool that tracks both the relational and structural dynamics of an investor's network may need to be developed. We also propose a new role to be developed for an investor organization—the head of social capital, a role that manages the relationships of institutional investors with clear guidelines and objectives for those relationships.

Social Capital Manager (Head of Social Capital)

The development of an organization's social capital is a different process from the development of human capital, which suggests that a unique role may be required by an investor organization. The idea of a social capital manager (SCM) was introduced in Chapter 2 as a dedicated role that institutional investors can use to facilitate their relationship-building capabilities. At a general level, the SCM would be in charge of the external relationships (social capital) of the investor organization for building organizational capacity and accessing special opportunities predominantly in the private-market space within and beyond existing investment themes and sectors.

The SCM would be someone who can develop relationships as well as match people from inside their own institution with people from outside in a way that adds value for all parties. The SCM would need to have intimate knowledge of the institution and a deep understanding of long-term investing and its value drivers. The SCM would also need a wide network of contacts from which to design and build opportunities (e.g. deal flow, co-investments, access, information, talent, and insights). The SCM would likely be part of a strategy division of an organization and vary in function depending on the type of investor.

An effective network can help address the various challenges associated with in-sourcing, such as origination, analysis, execution, monitoring, and even asset management. An appetite for in-sourcing really must then be accompanied by a clear collaboration plan, which would need to be developed by the SCM. This plan would need to outline the purpose and objectives of possible collaborations, whether for co-investment, collaboration, or co-operation.

The exact function of the SCM would depend on the size of investor organization. For “Very Large” and “Mega” investors, the SCM would be in charge of managing the relationships of potential co-investment partners. Having someone dedicated to manage these relationships will help build the trust required to translate the relationships into meaningful co-investment partnerships. The SCM would need to do deep research into the drivers of potential peers and assess the potential strengths or weaknesses of partnering with these organizations. Having a good grasp of the strategic direction of the investment teams within the organization would be required to know when opportunities might come up for raising capital and forming partnerships with peers. While forming relationships with specific management teams or development companies would likely be the responsibility of specific investment managers in the organization, the SCM can facilitate this process by identifying and examining potential candidates that the investment team may not know about. This would be crucial in order to reduce the time burden for the investment team, who may not have the bandwidth to explore these opportunities.

In developing relationships with potential co-investment peers, the SCM mirrors the role that relationship managers may play in placement firms or on the sales team of asset management firms. The SCM would also contribute to deal flow management or origination in areas that the specific investment teams do not have a grasp over or do not have the time and resources to look out for. The function of the SCM, as described previously, would require that the investor organization have an active strategy for co-investing with peers or for setting up collaborative investment vehicles. Thus, this description of the SCM role would pertain to “Very Large” or “Mega” type investors.

For “Medium” or “Large” investors, the function of the SCM may be different. Here the SCM may play a wider role, using social capital to help improve more than one aspect of the organization. These investors may place more emphasis on cooperation and collaboration. The idea would be to work with others to build generic organizational capacity. Because of the smaller size of these investors, it would be important for the SCM to develop relationships with the larger investors that are setting up the collaborative investment vehicles. This would require an understanding of the unique characteristics of the organization and compatibility that would appeal to the larger peers for inclusion. Relationship building with peers specific to the organization's collaborative objectives and sourcing of deal flow by the SCM would be more pertinent for these organizations, where the bandwidth of investment managers and other resources may be a lot more limited.

Complementary to the role of the SCM would be the need to organize relationships using some technology or software that can dynamically manage the complexities and social aspects of the network being created. This relationship management system would be a software intranet system that would help coordinate the relationships of employees across the organization. Such a system would be useful for all employees by documenting the history of relationships with certain peers, who key contacts are, and what issues others in the organization would most like to raise. The system would enable the organization to capture relationships made by individuals and dynamically track them even if the individual in charge left the organization.

With the preceding job description, the SCM would require a diverse set of skills. First, having a command of the organization would mean having a strong track record in finance with knowledge and experience in asset allocation, transaction execution, and investment analysis (knowing how performance measures/valuations are calculated). Being able to understand the impact of macroeconomic features on portfolio performance as well as sectoral trends would also be crucial. Importantly, the SCM would need to have a broad perspective of the organization and industry to understand where value can be created. Having a strong investment track record would provide credibility when engaging in conversations with other potential investor collaborators.

Interpersonal skills are a prerequisite for the role of a SCM. An SCM would be constantly on the road, meeting with people and attending conferences. The interpersonal skills of an SCM would, however, be somewhat different from those of salespeople or in some cases investor relations personnel at investment management firms. The SCM would not just be about closing a sale. An SCM needs to have a deeper empathy of what motivates potential long-term partners, be very good at reading people, and develop relationships well enough to be able to be frank about decisions and strategies. As identified earlier, trust and long-term partnership characterize the types of relationships sought after. SCMs would need to approach the role holding those values strongly.

As mentioned earlier, origination of opportunities and obtaining sources of deal flow are also crucially important factors that an investor's network can assist with. Just as an investment management firm relies on its relationships with various actors for its deal flow—receiving investment teasers from investment banks, hearing about opportunities from commercial bank capital restructurings, or building relationships with industry or sector specialists—SCMs can also help develop primary or secondary relationships that lead to various investment opportunities. An SCMs skill set would include being able to relate to a wide range of industries and make contact with potential sources of investment opportunities in diverse areas.

The role and skills of an SCM have perhaps been carried out already by various personnel in certain institutional investor organizations. For example, the CEO or CIO of an asset owner not only may bring existing relationships with them to the role but is usually invited to the most important meetings and gatherings of peer investors. While the CEO may bring a lot of social capital to an investor organization, the CEO may not be able to manage the social capital in an effective way. Someone who works closely with the CEO to manage these relationships and understands how the social capital can translate into material benefits for the organization is needed. As such, this person needs to also liaise with investment managers to ensure that attractive opportunities are seen by the right people in the organization. One of the roundtable initiatives specifically set up for co-investing was not as effective because the personnel present were too high-level and not the specific investment managers who could sign a check for co-investing with a peer.

The organizational structure of different investor organizations may also cause stumbling blocks to collaboration. For example, the international investment team of one investor may not be as important for an international peer who may be interested in learning from the domestic team, which has specific domestic expertise. An SCM who has greater oversight and the ability to directly connect the right managers together could be useful in this sense. Perhaps the most important aspect is to ensure that a healthy, collaborative environment is maintained within an investment organization so that ideas and contacts are shared seamlessly. The SCM may help facilitate such an environment.

While the role may not specifically be called an SCM, certain organizations already have incorporated a variant of the role described here. For example, as observed in Chapter 4, CPPIB used a consultant to help the organization identify and build relationships with possible investment partners in India. OMERS could have used the services of an SCM when they were developing relationships for the GSIA without detrimentally affecting the existing relationships that Borealis had with its investors. Other organizations have also tried to embark on a relationship-building exercise or conducted analysis on peer organizations. We suggest that a dedicated SCM can help coordinate and develop the strategy in a systematic and structured way.

Intermediaries of the Future

As indicated throughout this book, one of the competitive advantages of investment intermediaries, such as consultants, investment banks, investment management firms, and placement agents, is their deeply networked relationships with both sides of the investment management process. Their position within interorganizational networks enables them to match buyers of investment opportunities with those looking for financial capital to fund their businesses or projects. In essence, investment intermediaries are network creators and they intentionally occupy the "structural holes," which connect two separate groups of network actors possessing nonredundant information, to fulfill their brokerage roles. While financial service firms perform many other functions and are likely to exist for some time, the way institutional investor capital has been deployed is changing, and certain financial intermediaries will need to restructure their business models in order to accommodate the change.

In this book, we have specifically defined how more alignment can be achieved between investors and their agents and also examined some of the new vehicles that have been developed to facilitate more efficient capital deployment into private-market asset classes. A lot of the discussion has centered on the arrangement for pooling capital together for the buy side of the investment management process. The extensive discussion of institutional investor innovation and how such investors can collaborate, co-invest, and engage in more relational type of investment partnerships leads to a complementary discussion of how the types of long-term, real assets can be sourced.

Developing an efficient, effective network can in part help bring attractive investment opportunities. However, just as platforms can be developed that bring investor capital together, opportunity or deal flow platforms could also be developed to help bring real assets to the long-term investors addressed in this book. A number of long-term private market assets require specific procurement from government bodies and expensive bid processes, which can make them difficult to access for some investors. If procurement bodies understood the value that this group of long-term investors brings to their investment opportunities, a lot of the inefficiencies of traditional market-based exchanges could be avoided.

Infrastructure has featured as a prominent asset class case study throughout this book and provides another example of where such a deal platform could be implemented. Infrastructure assets are essentially public assets that are being transferred to the private sector for a variety of reasons. The procurement process is usually instigated entirely by the public sector. A platform that provides a pipeline of packaged investment opportunities for long-term investors would help reduce the inefficiencies and transaction costs in traditional private-market investing. Such a concept was coined by a group of state and provincial governments on the West Coast of North America—the West Coast Infrastructure Exchange (WCX). While the WCX is in its early stages of development, a number of interesting insights can be learned from its progress thus far.

The original purpose of the WCX was to identify opportunities for scaling regional and strategic publicly owned infrastructure, while also offering attractive investment opportunities for long-term investors. Two types of cooperation was needed for this to happen. First, the WCX needed to promote cooperation between local and state governments to share resources and reduce costs for procurement and ongoing monitoring. Second, the WCX needed to promote cooperation between the public and private sectors by providing investors with the necessary data to help identify and mitigate risks.[3]

The WCX aims to provide investors with project standards and evaluation tools that could contribute to the collection of data that is needed to integrate infrastructure with strategic asset allocation decisions. When the WCX is fully operational, it will develop a pipeline of investible projects and a database that would allow investors to search for and compare projects that need long-term private investment.

In a similar vein to the WCX, the Africa50 platform, created under the auspices of the African Development Bank, is a platform designed to shorten the time between an infrastructure project idea on the African continent and financial close. The platform aims to mobilize political support for necessary reforms and deploys skilled experts to work alongside the government. The Africa50 initiative has two main operations. First is the Project Development phase, whose primary aim is to increase the number of bankable infrastructure projects in Africa by providing legal, technical, and financial experts to projects at an early stage of development. Second, in the Project Finance phase, the initiative develops financing tools to provide investable products to investors for projects at different stages of their development.

Given the importance and value that can be created for the wider economy by long-term institutional investors, the idea of a platform that brings investment opportunities to investors could help facilitate the flow of capital into the real economy as opposed to being swallowed up by the fee-collecting financial services industry. The WCX provides an opportunity for slightly smaller institutional investors to gain access to attractive investments that fit their risk and return profile, the types of investments that more-sophisticated investors may find too efficient. Africa50 is an example of an initiative that works alongside governments to transform their potential infrastructure projects into reliable, robust financial products for institutional investors.

Another example, while not specifically a deal platform, is the recent White House–backed Aligned Intermediary, setup for the clean energy space in the United States. The Aligned Intermediary's core business is to source, screen, assess, diligence, audit, structure, syndicate, monitor, and de-risk clean- and green-technology opportunities, focusing on projects but also corporate investments. The idea is to connect green opportunities with aligned, return-seeking, commercial long-term institutional investors. Essentially, the Aligned Intermediary is a hub at the center of an ecosystem, pulling together various actors (government, national laboratories, regulators, universities) and capital types (institutional investors) to catalyze high-potential companies on the basis of commercial and impact objectives alone.

The aim of these initiatives is to develop sufficient internal expertise that would enable the platforms to not only successfully procure and issue investment opportunities but help provide the bridge between long-term institutional investors and the procuring bodies that are essentially the issuers of the assets. However, given the challenges institutional investors have experienced in attracting the right talent and expertise into their organizations,[4] it is debatable whether some of these organizations would be able to achieve their objectives in this area. One possible solution to this dilemma is for a separate organization that understands the investor community well to provide a bridge between investors and opportunities. In essence, such an organization would replace the role of an asset manager and provide a facilitating mechanism to bring the two parties together, a "platform to create platforms." Such an intermediary is conceptually shown in Figure 5.1.

The development of co-investment platforms and opportunity platforms may pave the way for the creation of a new type of intermediary that acts as an overarching, facilitating organization for the deployment of long-term institutional investor capital into private-market assets. The facilitating organization would help bring the two sides together in a way that investment banks and other financial intermediaries have done in the past. The main difference is that fees would not be so high, as the parties would have done most of the networking and deal structuring individually. The facilitating organization would need to develop strong relationships with long-term investor groups

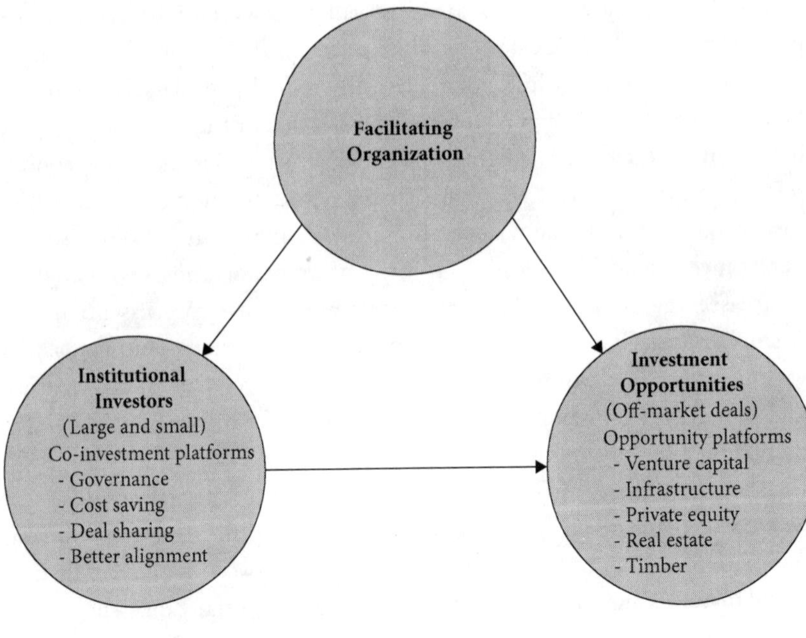

FIGURE 5.1 Facilitating organization structure

as well as opportunity platforms like the WCX. Some of the large think-tank organizations introduced in Chapter 2 such as the WEF, IIR, and PPI would be well positioned to fill this role. The facilitating organization would be an intermediary based on trusting relationships with long-term investors and procuring agencies. Such organizations are starting to form with the aid of technology platforms that connect a trusted group of investors with opportunities brought forward by the investors themselves. The idea is to extend this so that trusted procuring agencies can directly provide opportunities for the investors.

A final question on intermediaries for the future of long-term investment is how existing investment consultants, financial advisors, placement agents, and investment managers fit into the new trends emerging in this space. One thing for certain is that a remodeling or restructuring of the existing business models for some of these firms is required. For example, instead of investment consultants doing research on investment managers, these organizations could extend their capabilities to start appraising actual asset opportunities or use the knowledge gained in their work on investment managers to consult governments on how they can structure investable infrastructure products. Traditional financial and accounting consulting firms that already have relationships with institutional investors and governments for other services and have already developed a certain amount of trust could be used to provide deal sourcing and organizational building services to their clients. These firms would be well placed given their global presence and suite of services that they provide in general business and financial activities.

One key lesson from the co-investment platform case studies was the importance of the intermediator role and the requirement that this person or organization have sufficient investment and domain expertise without conflicts of interest. Financial advisors, placement agents, and investment consultants may all possess the domain expertise to carry out this role, but are they aligned? The big question is whether these organizations can be independent and not be captured by any one party driving the initiative forward. Other more boutique services firms and mainstream management consulting firms may also have a role to play. As indicated in Chapter 3, as investors get larger and more sophisticated, the investment services industry will likely become consolidated. Investors may need only complementary services such as those offered by consulting firms, in comparison to more expensive asset management firms. Existing firms will need to reconsider how their own models are likely to evolve as the private institutional investment industry continues to go through a re-intermediation process.

The Value of Long-Term Investing and the Role of Governments

The final actor that needs to be considered in the future of long-term investment is that of the public sector, including both central and local governments. The flow of capital into long-term real economy assets will require recognition from governments of the value that true long-term investors bring to society. Governments need to understand the value of partnering with true long-term investors as opposed to short-term transaction-oriented investors.

Along with the investment benefits that accrue to employees, citizens and taxpayer beneficiaries of these pension funds, sovereign funds, endowments, and family offices, long-term institutional investors executing long-term strategies create a pool of patient capital that can be invested in a broad range of productive assets that are essential to long-term sustainable economic development. The unique characteristics of long-term institutional investors make them vital sources of capital. There are several reasons why sovereign wealth funds, pension funds, endowments, foundations, and family offices can provide effective capital and outperform the broader market for real asset investing:

- **Time.** Most real assets have return profiles that can extend for decades, which can be a problem for a third-party manager. However, it isn't a problem for institutional investors with intergenerational objectives, such as family offices, sovereign funds, endowments, and pensions.
- **Scale.** Most real assets demand large check sizes, which can be problematic for third-party investors. A feature of large asset owners is their ability (and preference) to make large investments.
- **Liquidity.** Third-party managers are generally concerned with the liquidity of assets, especially as funds near the end of their lives. For true long-term investors, there is a greater ability to hold an investment for the life of the asset.
- **Social acceptance.** There is mounting pressure on state and local governments to find innovative sources of finance for their projects. This is forcing elected leaders to cultivate socially acceptable financing

> solutions. Pension funds, sovereign wealth funds, and foundations have local fiduciaries that would directly benefit from the investments and thus can provide an answer to these unique financing needs.

For these reasons, we believe that governments have a crucial role to play to help facilitate institutional investor capital into assets that are essential for long-term sustainable economic development. For example, a major risk of real asset investing centers on regulation and policy changes. In these cases, a government could treat a peer governmental investor differently than a generic private investor. Governments can play a role in identifying their true long-term investment partners and offer terms and conditions that are commensurate to a trusting, mutually dependent long-term relationship. This has started to happen in certain jurisdictions, where long-term investors are getting privileged access to assets by government entities.

In Australia, the Queensland government sold Queensland Motorways, a broken-down highway, bridge, and tunnel network, to the state's defined benefit pension fund manager, Queensland Investment Corporation (QIC) to satisfy pension liabilities. Through its operational improvements, QIC made a profit of several billion dollars on the sale of the assets, with the proceeds going back to the public-sector superannuation fund, benefiting the citizens of Queensland directly.

The National Investment and Infrastructure Fund (NIIF), announced by the Indian government in December 2015, is designed to leverage partnerships with other long-term investors for investing in Indian infrastructure. Abu Dhabi Investment Authority and Qatar Investment Authority have already signed MOUs to co-invest with the fund in India's infrastructure sector. The central Indian government will provide up to USD 3 billion per year to the fund and have a 49 percent stake, with other local and foreign long-term investors contributing a similar amount for a total of 51 percent equity. The objective is to maximize economic impact through infrastructure development in both greenfield and brownfield, stalled, and other nationally important projects.

In Quebec, Canada, the provincial government, which had been under pressure as the second-most indebted Canadian province with a large infrastructure investment gap, announced that it would hand over the planning, financing, and management of new infrastructure projects to the province's major pension fund, Caisse de Dépôt et Placement du Québec. Through the agreement, the pension fund has the discretion to select the projects that will help generate a commercial return for its clients. This example in Quebec illustrates how governments can form relationships with true long-term investment partners and provide privileged access to the benefit of its citizens and wider economy.

Final Thoughts

This book is not about high-level asset allocation or specific bottom-up investment strategies. Instead, it highlights the value to be captured by long-term investors, such as pension funds or sovereign wealth funds, from investing in their networks and relationships. Too many LTIs are complacent about their networks, expecting people and opportunities to simply come to them. We think that is a recipe for misalignment and underperformance.

A key motivation for our work has been the principal-agent issues that have surfaced between investors and investment managers and specifically the fees that significantly dampen the risk-adjusted rate of return for private investments. Structuring novel methods for deploying capital is a central purpose for this book.

The institutional investor universe currently stands at approximately $100 trillion and represents a diverse range of investor types. Larger, more sophisticated investors have already started to employ more-direct investment strategies for private markets, and as more funds grow to the necessary size, the number of funds going direct will likely increase. This has implications for the large asset management and financial services industry, as the number of managers used by a particular investor may decrease significantly. As a consolidation of investment managers takes place, these intermediaries in the investment management value chain will need to reconsider their models to keep them relevant in this evolving industry.

We would argue, however, that many members of the $100 trillion institutional investor universe are not exercising their competitive advantage of having scale and a long-term investment horizon when it comes to deploying capital. This book in many ways tries to help educate this large portion of institutional investor capital about the benefits of long-term private-market investing, and specifically how their more advanced peers have been structuring their investments in this area. Essentially, we help define the collaborative/partnership-based model of institutional investment, which has the objective of pooling capital together in a more-aligned fashion. Despite the fact that the investor universe is very diverse and that private-market assets are very heterogeneous, the collaborative model is proving to not only help institutional investors achieve their long-term investment objectives but also provide wider economic and social benefits.

APPENDIXES

1: Network Diagrams for Collaborative Vehicle Case Studies

2: Collaborative Models Database

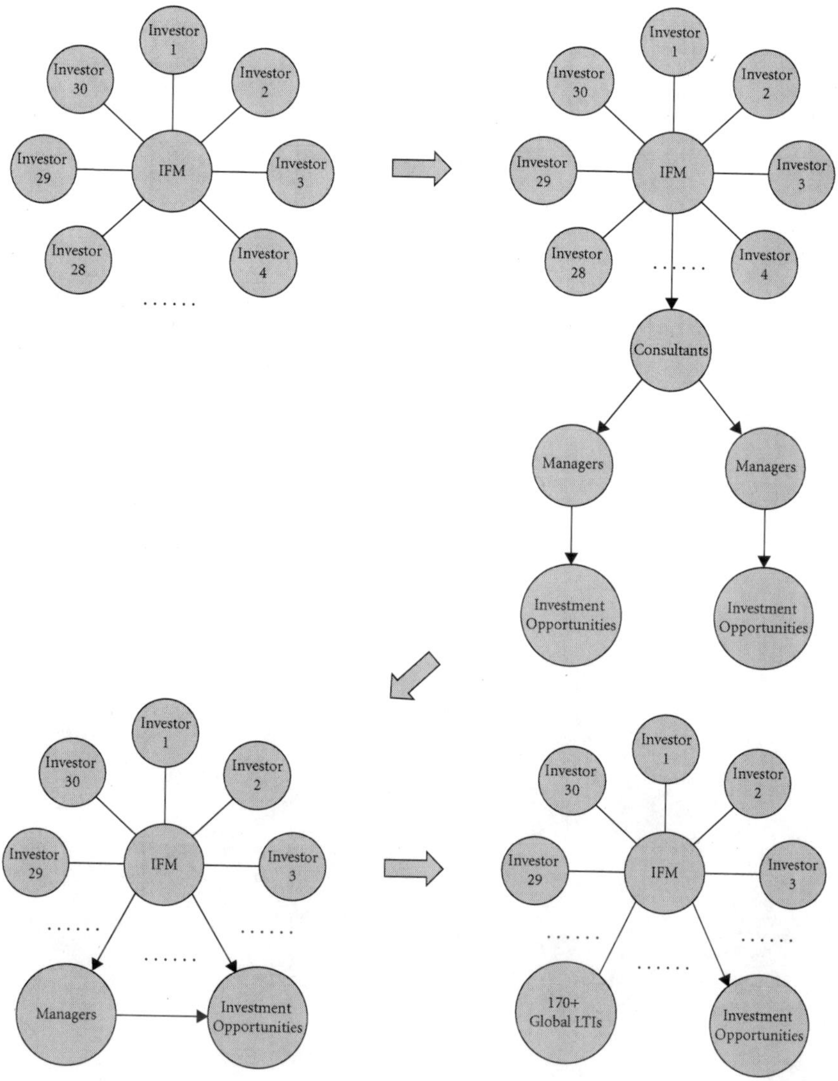

FIGURE A1.1 Network diagrams for IFM vehicle

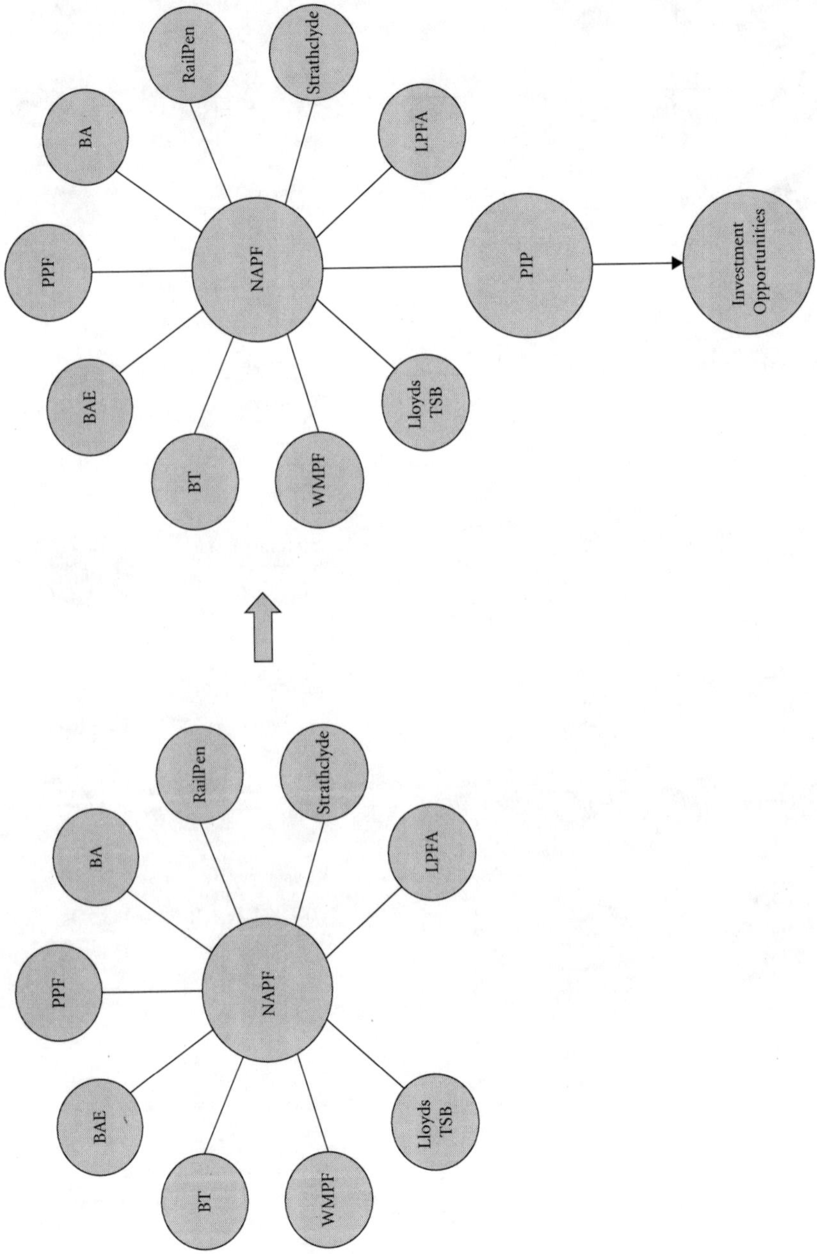

FIGURE A1.2 Network diagrams for PIP vehicle

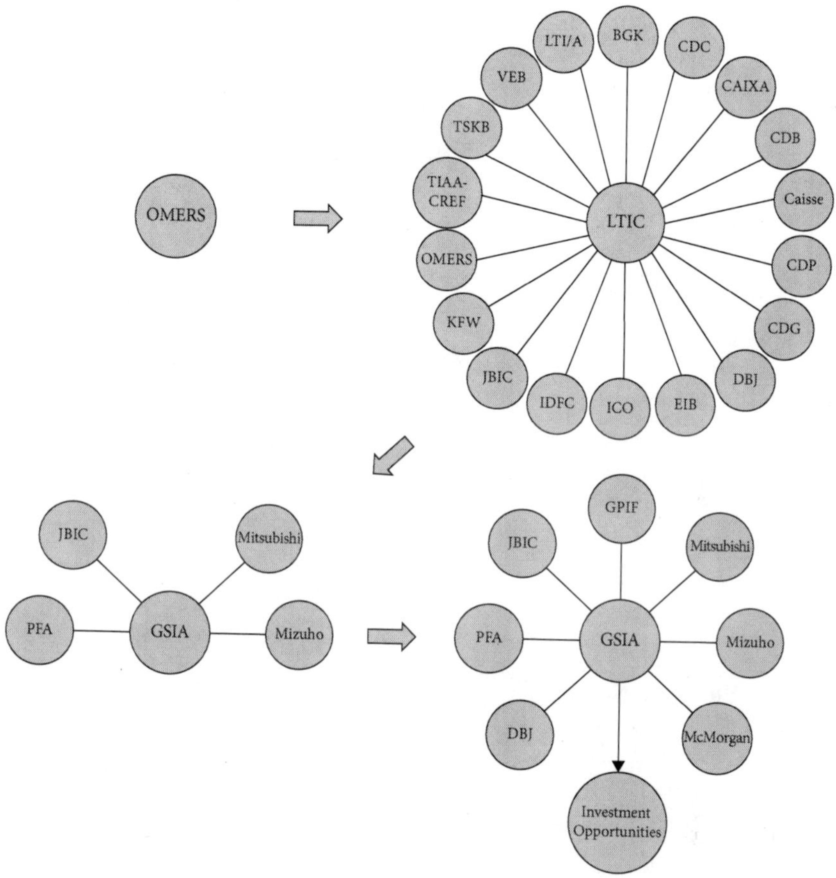

FIGURE A1.3 Network diagrams for GSIA vehicle

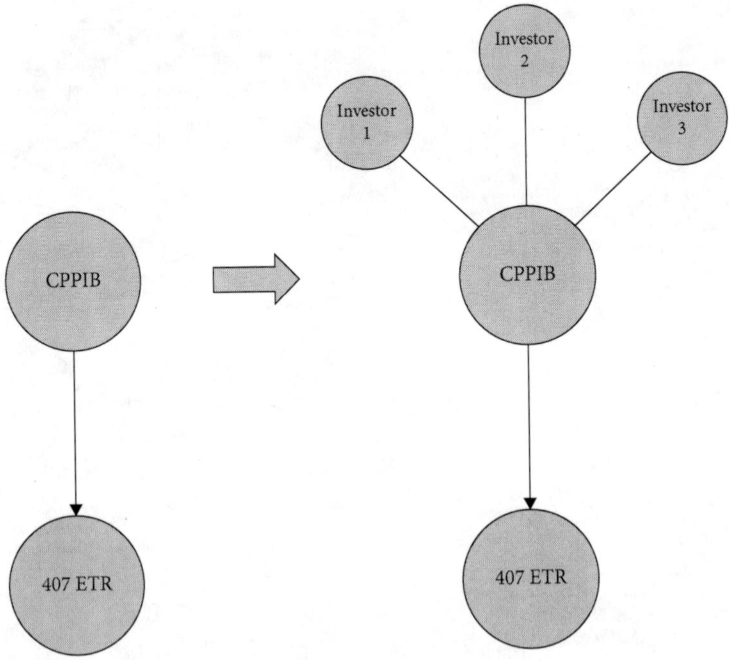

FIGURE A1.4 Network diagrams for CPPIB syndicate vehicle

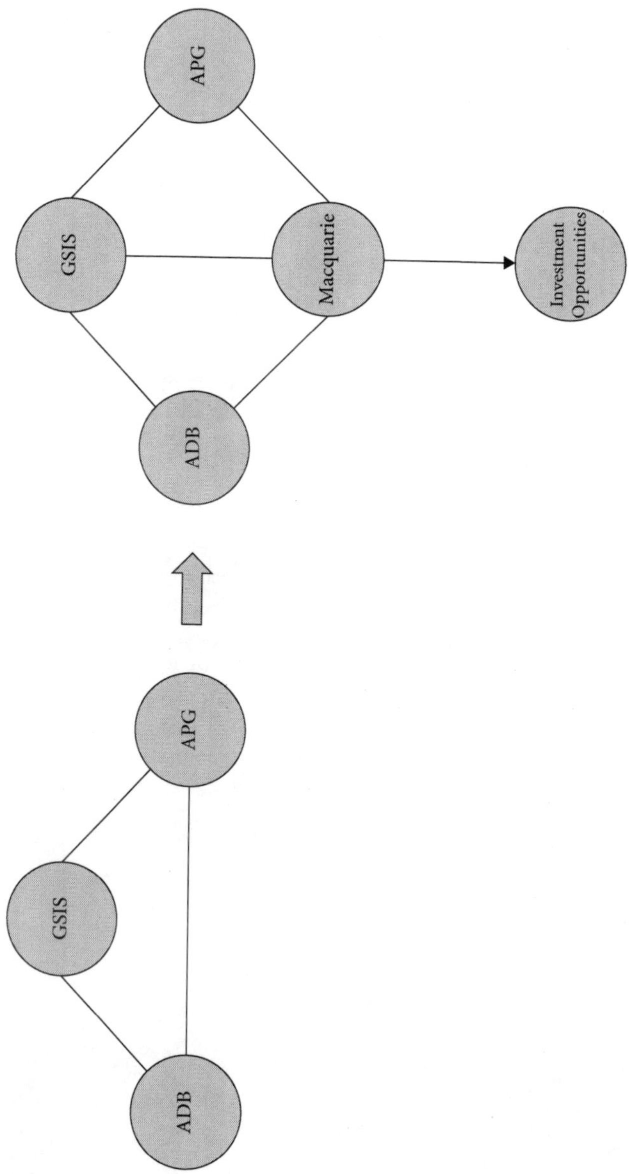

FIGURE A1.5 Network diagrams for PINAI vehicle

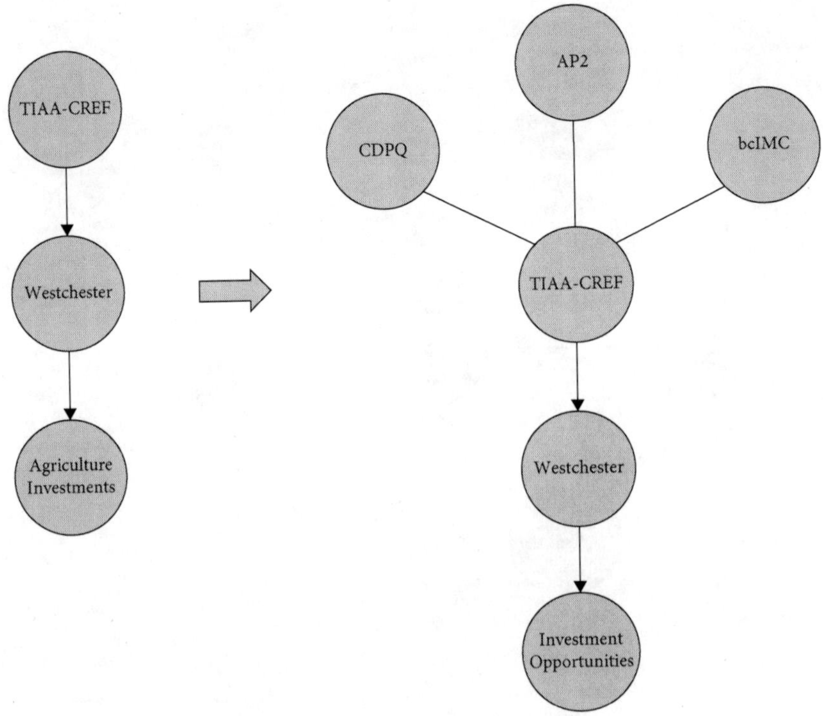

FIGURE A1.6 Network diagrams for TIAA-CREF vehicle

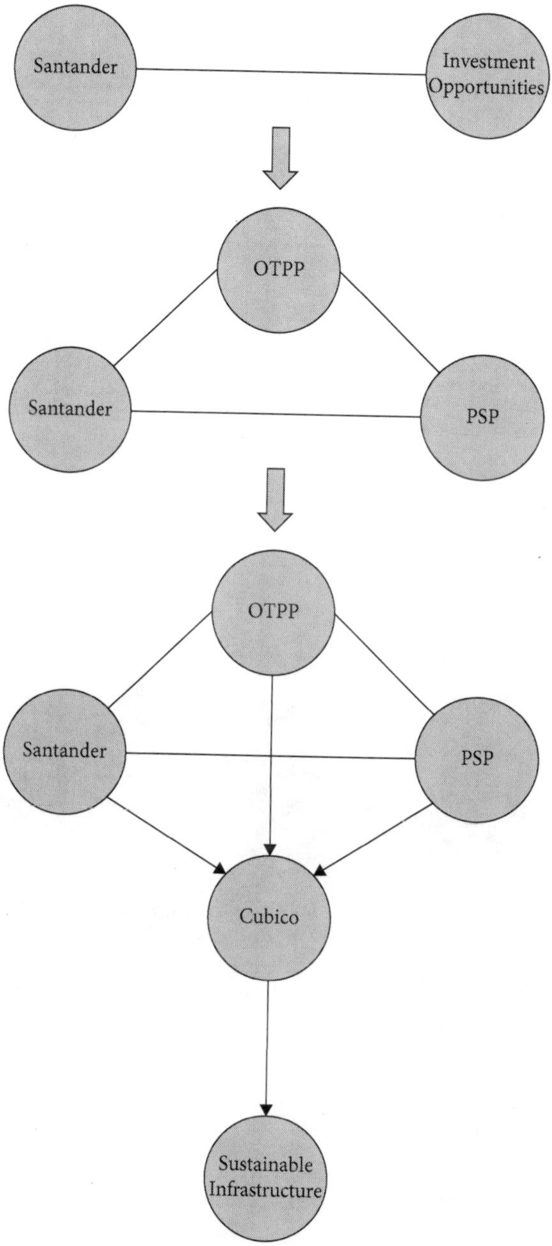

FIGURE A1.7 Network diagrams for Cubico vehicle

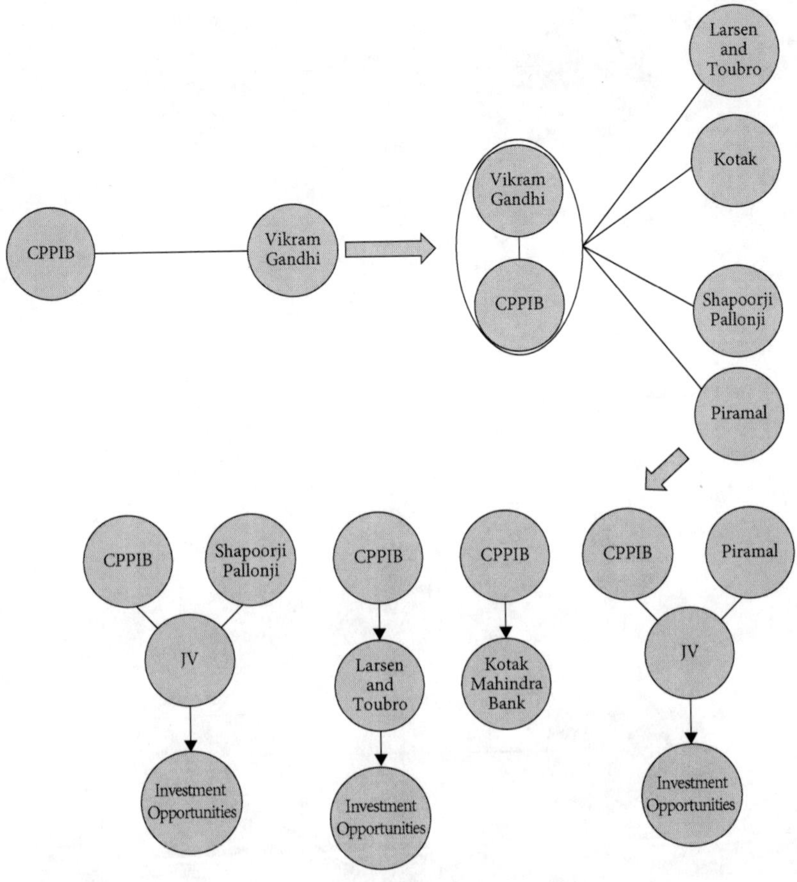

FIGURE A1.8 Network diagrams for CPPIB Indian vehicles

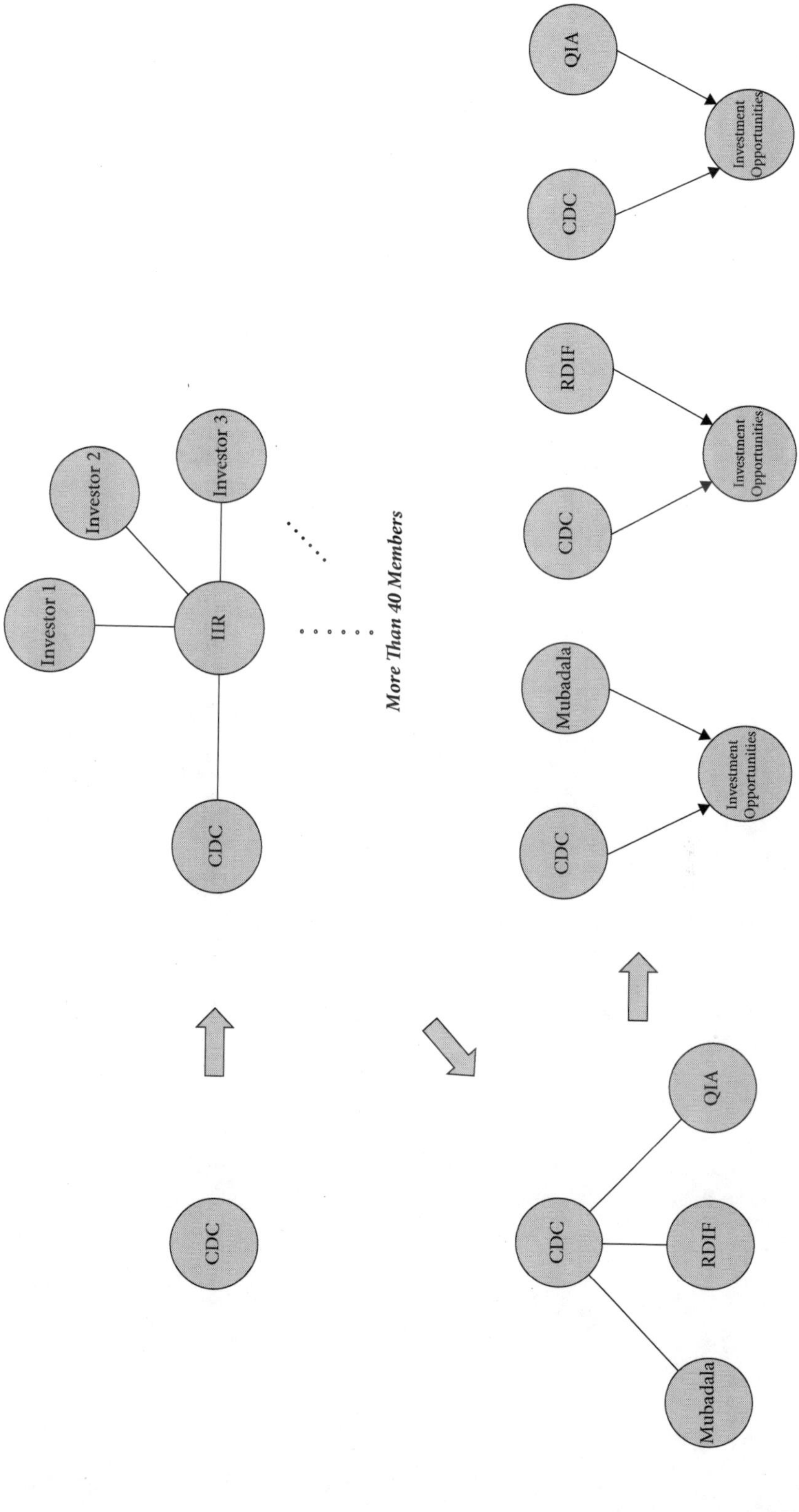

FIGURE A1.9 Network diagrams for CDC co-investment vehicles

TABLE A2 Collaborative models database

Name	*Type*	*No. of investors*	*Year founded*	*Size*	*Lead investor*	*Geography*	*Sector*
CPPIB 407 ETR	Co-investment vehicle	2	2010	$3.5 billion	CPPIB	Toronto	Road infrastructure
CPPIB Perimra	Co-investment vehicle	2	2013	$5.3 billion	CPPIB	Global	Technology
GIC Ascendas	Co-investment vehicle	2	2013	$483 million	GIC	India	Real estate infrastructure
GSIA	Co-investment vehicle	5	2012	$12.5 billion	OMERS	North America/ Europe	Infrastructure
Infraestructura Mexico	Co-investment vehicle	6	2015	$2.1 billion	CDPQ	Mexico	Road infrastructure
KG Co-invest	Co-investment vehicle	2	2015	CalPERS has $147 million committed	Blackstone	Global	Diversified
Mubadal RDIF	Co-investment vehicle	2	2013	$2 billion	RDIF	Russia	Diversified
PINAI	Co-investment vehicle	4	2012	$625 million	GSIS	Philippines	Infrastructure
RDIF KIA	Co-investment vehicle	2	2012	$500 million	RDIF	Russia/South Korea	Diversified
Alligned Intermediary	Co-investment vehicle/platform	4	2016	$960 million	University of California Regents	Global	Resource innovation
Astrea II	Co-investment vehicle/platform	7	2014	Unspecified	Temasek	Global	Diversified
Innovation Alliance	Co-investment vehicle/platform	3	2012	Unspecified	NZ Super	Global	Diversified
IST3 Global Infrastruktur (Swiss)	Co-investment vehicle/platform	6	2014	$276 million	ITS	OECD Member States	Infrastucture

(continued)

TABLE A2 Collaborative models database (*continued*)

Name	*Type*	*No. of investors*	*Year founded*	*Size*	*Lead investor*	*Geography*	*Sector*
Wessal Capital	Co-investment vehicle/platform	5	2011	\$3.4 billion	Ithmar Capital	Morocco	Real estate/ infrastructure
1411 Broadway	JV	2	2012	\$720 million	CDPQ	New York	Real estate holdings
330 Hudson	JV	3	2014	\$300 million	CDPQ	New York	Real estate holdings
ACH Limited Partnership	JV	2	2007	Unspecified	Abitibi Consolidated	Ontario	Energy infrastructure
ADIA Hines	JV	2	2013	\$250 million	Hines	India	Real estate infrastructure
ADIA NWD	JV	3	2015	\$2.4 billion	ADIA	Hong Kong	Real estate infrastructure
ADIA PSP	JV	2	2015	\$3.15 billion	ADIA	U.S.	Real estate infrastructure
ADIC Federation Centres	JV	2	2013	\$600 million	ADIC	Australia	Real estate holdings
ADIC Finchatton	JV	2	2013	\$1.2 billion	ADIC	London	Real estate holdings
ADIC-UBS Infrastructure Fund 1	JV	2	2008	\$500 million	ADIC	MENA	Real estate infrastructure
Agropur Cooperative	JV	6	2014	\$470 million	CDPQ	Canada	Dairy
AMMROC	JV	2	2010	\$800 million	Mubadala	UAE	Defense
APG Piramal	JV	2	2014	\$1 billion	Piramal	India	Infrastucture
APG Xander	JV	2	2016	\$450 million	APG	India	Real estate
Aventicum Capital Management	JV	2	2015	Unspecified	QIA	Europe	Asset management
BT HoldCo	JV	2	2015	\$5 billion	Bombadier	Global	Transport infrastructure

CCSB/Medini (Formerly Node 1)	JV	4	2007	$1.2 billion	Mubadala	Iskandar Region, Malaysia	Real estate infrastructure
CDC ZANTAZ	JV	2	2001	$10.9 million	CDC	France	Technology
CDCIC KHC	JV	2	2015	$200 million	CDCIC	Saudi Arabia	SMEs
CDPQ CPPIB	JV	2	2013	Unspecified	CPPIB	Canada	Real estate holdings
Centre for Agri-Bioscience	JV	2	2013	$23.5 million	Plenary	Melbourne	Real estate holdings
Cogeneration Belle Etoile	JV	3	2015	$13.7 million	CDC	France	Energy infrastructure
CP Logistics	JV	2	2015	$400 million	CalSTRS	U.S.	Real estate holdings
CPPIB E-shang	JV	2	2015	$500 million	APG	South Korea	Real estate infrastructure
CPPIB GECRE	JV	2	2013	$400 million	CPPIB	Tokyo	Real estate infrastructure
CPPIB GLP	JV	5	2015	$3.3 billion	CPPIB	U.S.	Real estate infrastructure
CPPIB Hermes	JV	2	2013	$501 million	CPPIB	U.K.	Real estate infrastructure
CPPIB Lend Lease	JV	3	2012	$2.9 billion	Lend Lease	Sydney	Real estate infrastructure
CPPIB Piramal	JV	2	2014	$500 million	CPPIB	India	Residential infrastucture
CPPIB Shapoor-ji-Palonji	JV	2	2013	$250 million	CPPIB	India	Office infrastructure
CPPIB/Land Securities	JV	2	2012	$1.4 billion	CPPIB	London	Real estate infrastructure

(continued)

TABLE A2 Collaborative models database (*continued*)

Name	*Type*	*No. of investors*	*Year founded*	*Size*	*Lead investor*	*Geography*	*Sector*
Data Core LP	JV	2	2012	$500 million	CalSTRS	U.S.	Real estate infrastructure
Fifth Street Properties	JV	2	pre-2002	$1.5 billion	Common-Wealth Partners	U.S.	Real estate infrastructure
FSI Investimenti	JV	2	2014	$2.2 billion	FSI	Italy	Diversified
GIC Brigade	JV	2	2014	$225 million	GIC	South India	Residential infrastructure
GIC DLF	JV	2	2015	$300 million	GIC	New Delhi	Real estate infrastructure
GIC Scentre	JV	2	2014	$1.6 billion	Scentre	New Zealand/ Australia	Real estate infrastructure
Institu-tional Mall Investors	JV	2	2003	Unknown	MCA	U.S.	Real estate infrastructure
Institutional Multifamily Partners	JV	2	2010	At least $1 billion	GID	U.S.	Real estate infrastructure
Ivanhoe TPG	JV	2	2013	$376 million	CDPQ	London	Real estate holdings
LCLC	JV	3	2015	$400 million	LOGOS China	China	Real estate infrastructure
London Array 1	JV	2	2014	$1.8 billion	DONG Energy	London	Energy infrastructure
MerchCap Solutions	JV	3	2013	$2 billion	Stonepoint	Global	Capital markets
MMC-Dubai World	JV	3	2007	$4.6 billion	Dubai World	Malaysia	Real estate infrastructure
Mubadala CDC	JV	2	2014	$300 million	Mubadala	France	Diversified
Mubadala GE	JV	2	2015	Unspecified	Mubadala	Al Ain	Aerospace

Mubadala Krisenergy	JV	2	2013	Unspecified	Mubadala	Thailand	Oil and gas
Mubadala Petrofac	JV	2	2008	Unspecified	Mubadala	UAE	Oil and gas
Mubadala UBG	JV	2	2008	Unspecified	Mubadala	Malaysia	Oil and gas
Mubadala Veolia	JV	2	2008	Unspecified	Veolia	MENA	Water infrastructure
NYSCRF Hines	JV	2	2011	$1 billion	Hines	U.S.	Real estate infrastructure
NYSCRF Metlife	JV	2	2016	$1.4 billion	Metlife	U.S.	Real estate infrastructure
PanCal	JV	2	2011	$1.15 billion	CalSTRS	U.S./Canada	Industrial infrastructure
ParkCal	JV	2	2015	$200 million	CalSTRS	U.S.	Real estate infrastructure
Penn West CIC	JV	2	2010	$3.2 billion	Penn West	Northern Alberta	Bitumen (asphalt) assets
PSP Aviva	JV	2	2015	Unspecified	PSP	London	Real estate
PSP Crestpoint H&R	JV	3	2014	$1.4 billion	PSP	North America	Real estate
PSP Reliance	JV	2	2015	$2.25 billion	Reliance Infrastructure	Mumbai, India	Electricity infrastructure
PSP Segro	JV	2	2011	$2.6 billion	PSP	Continental Europe	Logistics
QFIF	JV	2	2013	$330 million	CDC	France	Emerging companies
QIA Ascott	JV	2	2015	$600 million	QIA	Tokyo	Real estate infrastructure

(continued)

TABLE A2 Collaborative models database (*continued*)

Name	*Type*	*No. of investors*	*Year founded*	*Size*	*Lead investor*	*Geography*	*Sector*
QIA Douglas	JV	2	2016	$1.3 billion	QIA	Los Angeles	Real estate holdings
QIA RMZ	JV	2	2013	$300 million	QIA	India	Real estate infrastructure
RDIF PIF	JV	2	2015	$10 billion	RDIF	Russia	Infrastructure, agriculture
Temasek Khazanah	JV	2	2011	$9.8 billion	Khazanah	Malaysia/ Singapore	Real estate infrastructure
TIAA-CREF AP1 AP2	JV	3	2015	$2.2 billion	TIAA-CREF	Europe	Office infrastructure
TIAA-Cref CNP	JV	2	2013	$1.2 billion	TIAA-CREF	Germany	Commercial real estate
TPG/CalSTRS Austin LLC	JV	2	2012	$859 million	CalSTRS	Austin	Real estate holdings
University House Communities Group	JV	3	2016	$1.4 billion	GIC	U.S.	Real estate infrastructure
Waterford at Blue Lagoon	JV	2	2015	$374.5 million	TIAA-CREF	Miami	Residential infrastucture
Windsor Columbia Realty Fund	JV	2	2010	Unknown	GID	U.S.	Real estate infrastructure
Canary Wharf Group	JV/platform	2	2015	$3.9 billion	QIA	London	Real estate infrastructure
Cognit	JV/platform	2	2015	Unspecified	Mubadala	MENA	Technology
Cubico	JV/platform	3	2015	$2 billion	Santander	Global	Sustainable infrastructure
IQ Made in Italy	JV/platform	2	2012	$2.2 billion	FSI	Italy	Diversified
Mubadala Trafigura	JV/platform	2	2015	$1 billion	Mubadala	Spain	Mining

QIA CITIC	JV/platform	2	2014	$10 billion	QIA	Asia	Diversified
QIA KIC	JV/platform	2	2014	$2 billion	QIA	Qatar/SE Asia	Diversified
QIA RDIF	JV/platform	2	2014	$2 billion	RDIF	Russia/Qatar	Diversified
RCIF	JV/platform	2	2012	$3–4 billion	RDIF	Russia/China	Diversified
RKIP	JV/platform	2	2013	$500 million	RDIF	Russia/Korea	Diversified
Temasek JTC	JV/platform	2	2015	$5 billion	Temasek	Singapore	Real estate infrastructure
VEB RDIF JBIC	JV/platform	3	2013	$1 billion	RDIF	Russia/Japan	Diversified Russia-Japan
CalSTRS APG	Platform	3	2015	$500 million	CalSTRS	North America	Infrastructure
CDC IC	Platform	1	2014	$1 billion	CDC	Global	Diversified
CDPQ Empresas ICA	Platform	2	2015	$546 million	CDPQ	Mexico	Transport infrastructure
CDPQ Infrastructure	Platform	1	2015	$2.1 billion	CDPQ	Quebec	Transport infrastructure
EDIC	Platform	3	2014	$7.4 billion (by 2018)	Mubadala	UAE	Defense
GRL	Platform	1	2009	Unspecified	OMERS	Canada	Oil and gas
IFM	Platform	30	1994	$39.8 billion	Development Australia Fund	Global	Infrastructure
Liberty Living Mgmt	Platform	1	2015	$1.5 billion	CPPIB	U.K.	Real estate infrastructure
Mubadala CDBC	Platform	3	2015	$10 billion	Mubadala	Global	Diversified
PIP	Platform	10	2012	$2.88 billion	NAPF	U.K.	Infrastructure
RFIF	Platform	2	2013	$1.1 billion	RDIF	Russia/France	Diversified
TCGA II	Platform	20	2015	$3 billion	TIAA-CREF	Global	Agriculture

(*continued*)

TABLE A2 Collaborative models database (*continued*)

Name	*Type*	*No. of investors*	*Year founded*	*Size*	*Lead investor*	*Geography*	*Sector*
Temasek Oberoi	Platform	2	2015	$51 million	Temasek	India	Real estate holdings
GTRCo	Platform	2	2015	$667 million	TIAA-CREF	North America/ Latin America/Europe/ Asia	Timber
TIAA-CREF Agriculture LLC (TCGA I)	Platform	5	2012	$2 billion	TIAA-CREF	Global	Agriculture
TIAA Henderson	Platform/co-investment vehicle	1	2015	$306 million	TIAA-CREF	U.S.	Real estate holdings

Notes

Chapter 1

1. We acknowledge that there are other long-term investment strategies also. This book focuses on investments in private-market asset classes.

2. World Bank 2015.

3. Throughout, we use the terms *institutional investors, long-term investors (LTIs),* and *asset owners* synonymously to represent the group of investors described in this paragraph. These investors essentially own the capital that they are deploying. They are the direct, legal representatives of the fiduciaries that they represent. This is in contrast to asset managers, who invest on behalf of clients and do not legally own the capital they invest.

4. Sovereign wealth funds can be further categorized as stabilization funds, savings funds, reserve investment funds, development funds, or pension reserve funds. Please see Al-Hassan et al. 2013 for more detailed descriptions.

5. These long-term investors are the focus, although we recognize that a number of concepts in this book may not apply to all types of investors because of their unique characteristics.

6. Harris et al. 2014, Axelson et al. 2013, Robinson and Sensoy 2013.

7. Andonov 2014.

8. MacIntosh and Scheibelhut 2012, Fang et al. 2015, Andonov 2014.

9. Harris et al. 2014, Axelson et al. 2013, Robinson and Sensoy 2013.

10. The endowment model is characterized by a large allocation to alternative assets such as private equity through external managers. The direct model is characterized by a large allocation to alternative assets using an internal team of investment managers. The endowment model was pioneered by David Swensen, CIO of the Yale endowment, while the direct model was pioneered by large Canadian pension funds

such as the Ontario Teachers' Pension Plan (OTPP), the Canada Pension Plan Investment Board (CPPIB), and the Ontario Municipal Employees Retirement System (OMERS). See Ambachtsheer (2012), Swensen (2009), and WEF (2014) for a detailed explanation of these models.

11. Haldane 2010.

12. See http://www.forbes.com/forbes/2009/0316/080_harvard_finance_meltdown.html.

13. WEF 2011.

14. Lagarde 2011.

15. Della Croce et al. 2011.

16. Barton and Wiseman 2014.

17. Clark 2000.

18. Sharma 2012.

19. Morley 2002.

20. United Nations 2008.

21. Solow 1956.

22. Romer 1986, Lucas 1988, Aschauer 1989.

23. Munnell 1992, Gramlich 1994, Lau and Sin 1997, Berechman et al. 2006.

24. Kortum and Lerner 2000.

25. Timmons and Bygrave 1986, Samila and Sorenson 2011, Kortum and Lerner 2000.

26. Hagerman et al. 2005.

27. Temasek Holdings (Singapore): 18 percent IRR over 40 years; Khazanah Nasional (Malaysia): 13 percent IRR since 2004; Public Investment Corporation (South Africa): 16 percent IRR since 2004. Source: Annual reports of respective organizations.

28. TIAA-CREF 2012.

29. WEF 2011.

30. Ibid.

31. Laverty 1996.

32. Stoughton et al. 2011.

33. Warren 2014.

34. Irving 2009.

35. See Warren (2014) for a summary of behavioral and psychological influences on short-term behavior.

36. WEF 2011.

37. Ibid.

38. Towers Watson 2015b.

39. http://www.bloomberg.com/news/articles/2014-04-07/bogus-private-equity-fees-said-found-at-200-firms-by-sec.

40. http://fortune.com/2015/09/04/calpers-still-cant-get-out-of-its-own-way-on-private-equity/.

41. Andonov 2014.

42. Harris et al. 2014, Axelson et al. 2013, Robinson and Sensoy 2013, Ljungqvist and Richardson 2003, Stucke 2011, Fisher and Hartzell 2013.

43. Harris et al. 2014.

44. Inderst 2009, Knight and Sharma 2016, Sharma and Knight 2016.

45. CEM Benchmarking Inc. collects data from institutional investors through yearly questionnaires. The data in this study uses detailed information on the strategic asset allocation and performance of institutional investors during 1990–2011

46. Preqin 2014a, Towers Watson 2015a.

47. Malkiel 2013, Kaplan and Schoar 2005, Franzoni et al. 2012, Ljungqvist and Richardson 2003.

48. Franzoni et al. 2012.

49. Ang 2014.

50. Sheffer and Levitt 2010.

51. Blake 2014.

52. Andonov 2014.

53. Gompers and Lerner 2000, Metrick and Yasuda 2010, Fang et al. 2015.

54. Inderst 2009.

55. Torrance 2009, Sharma 2013.

56. http://www.wsj.com/articles/dutch-pension-fund-demands-full-fee-disclosure-from-private-equity-firms-1438850122.

57. Clark and Monk 2013.

58. Dai 2014.

59. Clark and Urwin 2008.

60. The Korea Investment Corporation experienced difficulty in doing direct deals because of insufficient knowledge within a particular sector and insufficient risk management practices. See http://www.wsj.com/articles/korea-investment-corp-learns-hard-lesson-1413962015.

61. Clark and Monk 2012.

62. WEF 2014.

63. http://www.nytimes.com/2009/09/06/magazine/06Economic-t.html.

64. http://nationalinterest.org/article/the-last-temptation-of-risk-3091.

65. Granovetter 1985.

66. Granovetter and Swedberg 2001.

67. Ibid.

Chapter 2

1. Hochberg et al. 2007, Bygrave 1988, Sahlman 1990.

2. Eccles and Crane 1987.

3. Borgatti and Foster 2003, Brass et al. 2004, Parkhe et al. 2006, Zaheer et al. 2010.

4. Parts of Chapter 2 come from Feng et al. 2016.

5. A social actor can be either an individual or organization. As explained by Molm (2007, p. 3599): "the participants in social exchange, called actors, can be either individual persons or collective actors such as groups or organizations, and either specific entities or interchangeable occupants of structural positions. This insight,

along with the use of network concepts, allowed the theory to span different levels of analysis more successfully than earlier exchange theories."

6. Burt 1992.
7. Nahapiet and Ghoshal 1998.
8. Modigliani and Miller 1958, Brealey et al. 2006, Brettel et al. 2007.
9. Babus et al. 2009.
10. Ibid.
11. Batjargal and Liu 2004, Batjargal 2007, Baum and Silverman 2004, Gulati and Higgins 2003, Meuleman et al. 2009.
12. Lerner 1994.
13. Wilson 1968.
14. Sahlman 1990, Hochberg et al. 2007.
15. Nahapiet and Ghoshal 1998.
16. Clark and Monk 2013.
17. Zaheer et al. 2010, p. 66.
18. Ibid., p. 69.
19. Once an understanding of the network effects on the behavior and performance of one network actor is achieved, the next step would be to start thinking about the design of a collaborative investment network from the perspective of all the participating investors (such as through the eyes of an investor platform or roundtable facilitator).
20. WEF 2014.
21. Please see the following for a deeper explanation of power in social networks: Cook et al. 1983, Cook et al. 2006, Cook and Yamagishi 1992, Emerson 1962, 1972a, 1972b, Pfeffer 1972a, 1972b, 1972c, Pfeffer and Salancik 2003.
22. Casciaro and Piskorski 2005.
23. Bearman 1997, Ekeh 1974, Lévi-Strauss 1969, 1969, Malinowski 1922, Sahlins 1965a, 1965b.
24. Yamagishi and Cook 1993.
25. Jackson 2008.
26. Skyrms 2004.
27. Ibid.
28. Baumet al. 2000, Podolny 2005, Stuart et al. 1999.
29. Al-Kharusi et al. 2014.
30. This has also spawned the rise of certain intermediaries that can help governments understand the benefits of infrastructure procurement for facilitating these long-term investment partnerships. More details and examples are outlined in Chapter 5.
31. IFSWF 2016.
32. LTIC 2016.
33. Ibid.
34. As is the case with Clark and Monk (2013), the examples do not provide an exhaustive list of all initiatives available but do summarize the main current options.

Other initiatives of note include the Focusing Capital on the Long Term initiative founded by CPPIB and McKinsey & Co., the Rotman International Centre for Pension Management discussion forums at the University of Toronto, the International Pensions Conference, and the Institutional Limited Partners Association. At the time of writing, the Co-investment Roundtable of Sovereign and Pension Funds (CROSAPF) was formed as a practical collaboration platform, with its first roundtable held in September 2014 in Seoul.

35. This is not to discount the value of having asset managers and other organizations at the roundtables. Part of an effective network for asset owners is to develop aligned relationships with all types of organizations based on trust, enabling knowledge, and information sharing.

Chapter 3

1. Berk and Green 2004.
2. Malkiel 2013, Kaplan and Schoar 2005, Franzoni et al. 2012, Ljungqvist and Richardson 2003.
3. Steindl 2013, Baks and Benveniste 2010, Lerner et al. 2007, Torrance 2007, Knight and Sharma 2015.
4. Atherton 2010, John 2009.
5. Baks and Benveniste 2010, Anson 2012, Torrance 2009, and Steindl 2013 are examples.
6. Appelbaum and Batt 2016.
7. Ibid.
8. Ibid.
9. Lewis 2015.
10. Ibid.
11. Appelbaum and Batt 2016.
12. Ibid.
13. Ibid.
14. Williamson 1979, Bradach and Eccles 1989, Gibbons 2010, Smyth 2014.
15. Bradach and Eccles 1989.
16. Williamson 1979, Macneil 1977.
17. In a fund structure, there is a vehicle, which is a legal construct—the most common models are the limited partnership, the limited company, and the unit trust. In a limited partnership, the partnership agreement both creates the fund vehicle and defines the contractual relationship between the fund operator and the investors. The fund operator then enters into a service agreement with the investment manager, who is usually an affiliate of the fund operator. Second, for a straightforward appointment of a fund manager by an investor to manage a segregated portfolio, a formal service contract defines the terms and conditions of the arrangement.
18. Some structural disadvantages also prohibit smaller pension funds from getting access to better-performing managers. For example, many public pension boards

demand that an external consultant vet a manager. But many consultants will take the time to vet a manager only if they can repackage and sell on a due diligence report. Therefore, consultants' own priorities can prevent underresourced and risk-averse pension funds from getting in early.

19. Stone 2005.

20. Gudel 1998.

21. Within law and economics literature, the classification and terminology of contracts is not used in a precise and consistent way. The spectrum used here draws upon some of the key ideas of Macneil and Williamson, who were the earliest observers of such a spectrum.

22. Campbell 2001.

23. Smyth 2014.

24. Williamson 1979.

25. Ibid.

26. Smyth 2014.

27. Campbell 2001, Macaulay 1963.

28. Williamson 1979.

29. Gudel 1998.

30. Campbell 2001.

31. Stone 2005.

32. Ibid.

33. Poppo and Zenger 2002.

34. Ibid.

35. Kimel 2005.

36. Macaulay 1963.

37. Henisz et al. 2012, Smyth 2014.

38. Smyth 2014.

39. Henisz et al. 2012, Gil 2009, Lee and Cavusgil 2006.

40. Uzzi 1997, Vargo and Lusch 2004.

41. Colledge 2005.

42. Quoting Macneil (1974): "To presentiate is to make or render present in place or time; to cause to be perceived or realized as present. Presentiation is only a manner in which a person perceives the future's effect on the present; but it depends upon events outside the individual psyche, events viewed as deterring the future."

43. Gil 2009.

44. Ghoshal and Moran 1996, Macaulay 1963.

45. McCahery and Vermeulen 2008.

46. Bernheim and Whinston 1998, Levin 2003, Kvaløy and Olsen 2005.

47. Mayer and Argyres 2004, Argyres et al. 2007, Poppo and Zenger 2002.

48. Adler 2001, Poppo and Zenger 2002.

49. Ibid.

50. Ibid.

51. Monk and Sharma 2016.

52. Crocker and Masten 1991.

53. Colledge 2005.

54. For example, relational governance norms may facilitate the formalization of the relationships between peer investors that are looking to form co-investment partnerships. Also, fund managers may develop relationships with investors first that then turn into a formal, more-aligned fund structure; that is, forming a network (using social network theory) is not independent of incorporating relational governance (both are needed to formulate investment partnerships).

55. Watson Wyatt 2009.

56. Ibid.

57. Preqin 2013.

58. Della Croce and Sharma 2014.

59. Depending on jurisdiction, this trend started to occur toward the end of the twentieth century as investors wanted to diversify their portfolios away from equity and fixed income markets.

60. Appelbaum and Batt 2016.

61. Ibid.

62. Bainbridge 2005.

63. Ang (2014) draws upon the general principle that "an asset manager needs to look more like an asset owner in order to act like one" when developing methods to achieve more alignment. Outcome-based contracts, which include bonuses to be paid if the manager outperforms a benchmark or peer group, enable the fund manager to share the principal's reward. Behavior-based contracts involve asset owners monitoring asset managers' behavior and closely restricting managers' opportunities to deceive investors. This may involve restricting certain investments but also rewarding certain efforts. Inference-based contracts would result in rewarding asset managers at disproportionately higher levels for unique outperformance, or disproportionately lower levels for outcomes that are likely only if they were negligent. This is based on the principle that nonlinear contracts are optimal. The type of arrangement adopted would depend on the overall manager selection and asset class strategy of the investor.

64. Termination at will could create distortions toward short-termism. The factors that drive termination would need to be spelled out. These termination provisions seem to exist for most public-market investments; however, it is a lot more difficult in private-market investments.

65. Appelbaum and Batt 2016.

66. Clark and Monk 2015, Jenkinson et al. 2015.

67. Approximated using the categories defined by the World Economic Forum in WEF (2014).

Chapter 4

1. Fang et al. 2015.

2. WEF 2014.

3. Fang et al. 2015, Beath 2015, Miller and Flynn 2010.

4. Preqin 2014b.

5. Kogut 1988.

6. Ibid.

7. Polanyi 1967.

8. Data for this case study come from the IFM website, www.ifminvestors.com, and from interviews with senior investment managers at pension funds located in Australasia.

9. See Appendix 1 for network figures.

10. Data for this case study come from interviews with senior managers at pension funds, lawyers, and consultants based in the United Kingdom as well as from publicly available sources.

11. PPF 2009.

12. NAPF 2015.

13. The founding pension fund members included BAE Systems, BT Pension Scheme, West Midlands Pension Fund, Pension Protection Fund, Lloyds TSB, British Airways Pensions, Railways Pension Scheme, Strathclyde Pension Fund, London Pensions Fund Authority, and one other anonymous fund.

14. The Henderson Infrastructure Fund provided a contrasting template for setting up an improved more aligned investment vehicle for the LPs. For more information regarding the Henderson Failure, see http://www.ipe.com/henderson-faces-lawsuit-from-30-pension-funds/36781.fullarticle.

15. Belt and Nimmo 2013.

16. HM Treasury 2013.

17. Belt and Nimmo 2013.

18. Jenkinson et al. 2015, Clark and Monk 2015.

19. Data for this case study come from interviews with senior executives at pension funds in Canada and from publicly available sources.

20. Jacobius 2014.

21. The CPPIB is a leading global professional investment management organization that invests the assets of the Canada Pension Plan not currently needed to pay benefits. It was established in December 1997 as a Canadian crown corporation responsible for managing the Canada Pension Plan, which approximately eighteen million Canadians contribute to or receive benefits from. The CPPIB manages over USD 200 billion in assets and has been applying the direct investment model in infrastructure since 2006.

22. Data for this case study come from public sources and interviews with senior managers at pension funds in Canada and London.

23. Dyck and Virani 2012.

24. Ibid.

25. Belt and Nimmo 2013.

26. Data for this case study come from public sources and interviews with global fund managers.

27. Della Croce and Sharma 2014.

28. Ibid.

29. Ibid., Asian Development Bank 2016.

30. The BT and BAE Systems Pension Fund and the London Pensions Fund Authority pulled out of the Pensions Infrastructure Platform (PIP) in February 2014.

31. Data for this case study come from interviews with senior investment managers at U.S.-based pension funds and the TIAA website: https://www.tiaa.org/public/assetmanagement/strategies/alternatives/agriculture.

32. Data for this case study come mainly from interviews with investment managers at pension funds in Canada and the United Kingdom and the Cubico website: http://www.cubicoinvest.com.

33. Data for this case study come from interviews with real estate development teams in India and from publicly available information.

34. Shapoorji Pallonji 2016.

35. Sarkar 2013, Sarkar and Sanjai 2014.

36. Data for this case study come from interviews with investment managers at sovereign wealth funds in France and the Middle East and from the CDC International Capital website: http://www.cdcicapital.fr/en/about.html.

37. These were the core relationships and makeup of the team at the time of writing, although further partnerships have been established subsequently with Korea Investment Corporation (KIC), China Investment Corporation (CIC), and Saudi Arabia–based Kingdom Holding Company (KHC).

Chapter 5

1. Dixon and Monk 2014.
2. Porteous 1999, Faulconbridge et al. 2007.
3. Hachigian 2014.
4. Dixon and Monk 2014.

Bibliography

Adler, Paul S. 2001. "Market, Hierarchy, and Trust: The Knowledge Economy and the Future of Capitalism." *Organization Science* 12 (2): 215–234.

Al-Hassan, Abdullah, Michael G. Papaioannou, Martin Skancke, and Cheng Chih Sung. 2013. "Sovereign Wealth Funds: Aspects of Governance Structures and Investment Management." Working Paper no. 13/231, International Monetary Fund, Washington, DC.

Al-Kharusi, Qais A., Adam D. Dixon, and Ashby H. B. Monk. 2014. "Getting Closer to the Action: Why Pension and Sovereign Funds Are Expanding Geographically." Available at SSRN: http://ssrn.com/abstract=2380277.

Ambachtsheer, K. 2012. "Norway vs. Yale . . . OR vs. Canada?—A Comparison of Investment Models." *The Ambachtsheer Letter.*

Andonov, A. 2014. "Pension Fund Asset Allocation and Performance." PhD dissertation, Maastricht University.

Ang, Andrew. 2014. *Asset Management: A Systematic Approach to Factor Investing.* Oxford: Oxford University Press.

Anson, Mark. 2012. "Asset Owners versus Asset Managers: Agency Costs and Asymmetries of Information in Alternative Assets." *Journal of Portfolio Management* 38 (3): 89–103.

Appelbaum, Eileen, and Rosemary Batt. 2016. *Fees, Fees and More Fees: How Private Equity Abuses Its Limited Partners and US Taxpayers.* Washington, DC: Center for Economic and Policy Research.

Argyres, Nicholas S., Janet Bercovitz, and Kyle J. Mayer. 2007. "Complementarity and Evolution of Contractual Provisions: An Empirical Study of IT Services Contracts." *Organization Science* 18 (1): 3–19.

Aschauer, David Alan. 1989. "Is Public Expenditure Productive?" *Journal of Monetary Economics* 23 (2): 177–200.

Asian Development Bank. 2016. "Philippine's PINAI Fund." http://www.adb.org/news/infographics/philippines-pinai-fund.

Atherton, Alison, James Lewis, and Roel Plant. 2007. "Causes of Short-Termism in the Finance Sector." Discussion paper, Institute of Sustainable Futures, University of Technology Sydney, Broadway, NSW.

Atherton, Pam. 2010. "Henderson Faces Lawsuit from 30 Pension Funds." *Investment & Pensions Europe* (September 7).

Axelson, U., M. Sorensen, and P. Strömberg. 2013. "The Alpha and the Beta of Private Equity." Working paper, Columbia University London School of Economics and University of Chicago.

Babus, Ana, Elena Carletti, and Franklin Allen. 2009. "Financial Crises: Theory and Evidence." Available at SSRN: http://ssrn.com/abstract=1422715.

Bachher, Jagdeep Singh, and Ashby H. B. Monk. 2013. "Platforms and Vehicles for Institutional Co-Investing." *Rotman International Journal of Pension Management* 6 (1): 64–71.

Bainbridge, Stephen M. 2005. "Shareholder Activism and Institutional Investors." Law-Econ Research Paper no. 05-20, UCLA School of Law.

Baker, George, Robert Gibbons, and Kevin J. Murphy. 2002. "Relational Contracts and the Theory of the Firm." *Quarterly Journal of Economics* 117 (1): 39–84.

Baks, Klaas P., and Lawrence M. Benveniste. 2010. "Alignment of Interest in the Private Equity Industry." Emory Center for Alternative Investments, Emory University Goizueta Business School, Atlanta, GA.

Barton, Dominic, and Mark Wiseman. 2014. "Focusing Capital on the Long Term." *Harvard Business Review* 92 (1/2): 44–51.

Batjargal, Bat. 2007. "Comparative Social Capital: Networks of Entrepreneurs and Venture Capitalists in China and Russia." *Management and Organization Review* 3 (3): 397–419.

Batjargal, Bat, and Mannie Liu. 2004. "Entrepreneurs' Access to Private Equity in China: The Role of Social Capital." *Organization Science* 15 (2): 159–172.

Baum, Joel A. C., Tony Calabrese, and Brian S. Silverman. 2000. "Don't Go It Alone: Alliance Network Composition and Startups' Performance in Canadian Biotechnology." *Strategic Management Journal* 21 (3): 267–294.

Baum, Joel A. C., and Brian S. Silverman. 2004. "Picking Winners or Building Them? Alliance, Intellectual, and Human Capital as Selection Criteria in Venture Financing and Performance of Biotechnology Startups." *Journal of Business Venturing* 19 (3): 411–436.

Bearman, Peter. 1997. "Generalized Exchange." *American Journal of Sociology* 102 (5): 1383–1415.

Beath, Alexander D. 2015. "Value Added by Large Institutional Investors between 1992–2013." CEM Benchmarking, Toronto.

Belt, Bradley D., and Joshua Nimmo. 2013. "Catalysing Pension Fund Investment in the Nation's Infrastructure." Research report, Milken Institute, Washington, DC.

Berechman, Joseph, Dilruba Ozmen, and Kaan Ozbay. 2006. "Empirical Analysis of Transportation Investment And Economic Development at State, County and Municipality Levels." *Transportation* 33 (6): 537–551.

Berk, Jonathan B., and Richard C. Green. 2004. "Mutual Fund Flows and Performance in Rational Markets." *Journal of Political Economy* 112 (6): 1269–1295.

Bernheim, B. Douglas, and Michael D. Whinston. 1998. "Incomplete Contracts and Strategic Ambiguity." *American Economic Review* 88 (4): 902–932.

Blake, D. 2014. "On the Disclosure of the Costs of Investment Management." Working paper, Cass Business School, London.

Borgatti, Stephen P., and Pacey C. Foster. 2003. "The Network Paradigm in Organizational Research: A Review and Typology." *Journal of Management* 29 (6): 991–1013.

Bradach, Jeffrey L., and Robert G. Eccles. 1989. "Price, Authority, and Trust: From Ideal Types to Plural Forms." *Annual Review of Sociology* 15 (1): 97–118.

Brass, Daniel J., Joseph Galaskiewicz, Henrich R. Greve, and Wenpin Tsai. 2004. "Taking Stock of Networks and Organizations: A Multilevel Perspective." *Academy of Management Journal* 47 (6): 795–817.

Brealey, R. A., S. C. Myers, and A. J. Marcus. 2006. *Fundamentals of Corporate Finance.* New York: McGraw-Hill/Irwin.

Brettel, Malte, Wolfgang Breuer, and Ingo Boehner. 2007. "The Syndication Network and Deal Flow of Venture Capital Firms." Available at SSRN: http://ssrn.com/abstract=1018388.

Burt, Ronald S. 1992. *Structural Holes: The Social Structure of Competition.* Cambridge, MA: Harvard University Press.

Bygrave, William D. 1988. "The Structure of the Investment Networks of Venture Capital Firms." *Journal of Business Venturing* 3 (2): 137–157.

Campbell, David. 2001. "Ian Macneil and the Relational Theory of Contract." In *The Relational Theory of Contract: Selected Papers of Ian Macneil*, edited by Ian R. Macneil. London: Sweet and Maxwell.

Casciaro, Tiziana, and Mikolaj Jan Piskorski. 2005. "Power Imbalance, Mutual Dependence, and Constraint Absorption: A Closer Look at Resource Dependence Theory." *Administrative Science Quarterly* 50 (2): 167–199.

CDC International Capital. 2016. "CDC International Capital." http://www.cdcicapital.fr/en/.

Clark, Gordon L. 2000. *Pension Fund Capitalism.* Oxford: Oxford University Press.

Clark, Gordon L., and Ashby H. B. Monk. 2012. "Principles and Policies for In-House Asset Management." *Journal of Financial Perspectives* 1 (3): 39–47.

———. 2013. "Transcending Home Bias: Institutional Innovation through Cooperation and Collaboration in the Context of Financial Instability." Available at SSRN: http://ssrn.com/abstract=2353364.

———. 2015. "The Contested Role of Investment Consultants: Ambiguity, Contract, and Innovation in Financial Institutions." Available at SSRN: http://ssrn.com/abstract=2613939.

Clark, Gordon L., and Roger Urwin. 2008. "Best-Practice Pension Fund Governance." *Journal of Asset Management* 9 (1): 2–21.

Coase, Ronald H. 1937. "The Nature of the Firm." *Economica* 4 (16): 386–405.

Cohen, Lauren, Andrea Frazzini, and Christopher Malloy. 2007. "The Small World of Investing: Board Connections and Mutual Fund Returns." NBER Working Paper no. 13121, NBER, Cambridge, MA.

Coleman, James S. 1988. "Social Capital in the Creation of Human Capital." *American Journal of Sociology* 94: S95–S120.

———. 1990. *Foundations of Social Theory.* Cambridge, MA: Harvard University Press.

Colledge, Barbara. 2005. "Relational Contracting: Creating Value beyond the Project." *Lean Construction Journal* 2 (1): 30–45.

Cook, Karen S., Coye Cheshire, and Alexandra Gerbasi. 2006. "Power, Dependence, and Social Exchange." *Contemporary Social Psychological Theories* (2006): 194–216.

Cook, Karen S., Richard M. Emerson, Mary R. Gillmore, and Toshio Yamagishi. 1983. "The Distribution of Power in Exchange Networks: Theory and Experimental Results." *American Journal of Sociology*: 275–305.

Cook, Karen S., and Toshio Yamagishi. 1992. "Power in Exchange Networks: A Power-Dependence Formulation." *Social Networks* 14, no. 3–4 (1992): 245–265.

Crocker, Keith J., and Scott E. Masten. 1991. "Pretia ex Machina? Prices and Process in Long-Term Contracts." *Journal of Law & Economics* 34 (1): 69–99.

Cubico. 2016. "Cubico Sustainable Investments." http://www.cubicoinvest.com.

Cummings, James R., and Katrina Ellis. 2015. "Risk and Return of Illiquid Investments: A Trade-Off for Superannuation Funds Offering Transferable Accounts." *Economic Record* 91 (295): 463–476.

Dai, S. 2014. "Korea Investment Corp. Learns Hard Lesson." *Wall Street Journal*, October 22.

Della Croce, R., and R. Sharma. 2014. "Pooling of Institutional Investors Capital—Selected Case Studies in Unlisted Equity Infrastructure." OECD Working Papers on Finance, Insurance and Private Pensions, OECD, Paris.

Della Croce, Raffaele, Fiona Stewart, and Juan Yermo. 2011. "Promoting Longer-Term Investment by Institutional Investors." *OECD Journal: Financial Market Trends* (1): 145–164.

Dixon, Adam D., and Ashby H. B. Monk. 2014. "Frontier Finance." *Annals of the Association of American Geographers* 104 (4): 852–868.

Dyck, Alexander, and Aazam Virani. 2012. "Buying into the 407: The Syndication Protocol as a New Model for Infrastructure Investing." *ICPM Case Study* 29, Rotman ICPM, Toronto.

Eccles, Robert G., and Dwight B. Crane. 1987. "Managing through Networks in Investment Banking." *California Management Review* 30 (1): 176–195.

Égert, Balázs, Tomasz J. Kozluk, and Douglas Sutherland. 2009. "Infrastructure and Growth: Empirical Evidence." Working paper.

Ekeh, Peter Palmer. 1974. *Social Exchange Theory: The Two Traditions.* Cambridge, MA: Harvard University Press.

Emerson, Richard M. 1962. "Power-Dependence Relations." *American Sociological Review* 27 (1): 31–41.

———. 1972a. "Exchange Theory, Part I: A Psychological Basis for Social Exchange." In *Sociological Theories in Progress*, edited by J. Berger et al., 38–57. Boston: Houghton-Mifflin.

———. 1972b. "Exchange Theory, Part II: Exchange Relations and Networks." In *Sociological Theories in Progress*, edited by J. Berger et al., 58–87. Boston: Houghton-Mifflin.

Fang, Lily, Victoria Ivashina, and Josh Lerner. 2015. "The Disintermediation of Financial Markets: Direct Investing in Private Equity." *Journal of Financial Economics* 116 (1): 160–178.

Faulconbridge, James, Ewald Engelen, Michael Hoyler, and Jonathan Beaverstock. 2007. "Analysing the Changing Landscape of European Financial Centres: The Role of Financial Products and the Case of Amsterdam." *Growth and Change* 38 (2): 279–303.

Feng, Wen, Rajiv Sharma, and Ashby H. B. Monk. 2016. "Designing an Institutional Investor's Collaborative Network: A Case Study of Value Network Analysis." Available at SSRN: http://ssrn.com/abstract=2832637.

Fisher, Lynn M., and David J. Hartzell. 2013. "Real Estate Private Equity Performance: A New Look." Working paper, Kenan-Flagler Business School, University of North Carolina at Chapel Hill.

Foa, Edna B., and Uriel G. Foa. 1980. "Resource Theory: Interpersonal Behavior as Exchange." In *Social Exchange: Advances in Theory and Research*, edited by Kenneth J. Gergen, Martin S. Greenberg, and Richard H. Willis, 77–94. New York: Plenum Press.

Franzoni, Francesco, Eric Nowak, and Ludovic Phalippou. 2012. "Private Equity Performance and Liquidity Risk." *Journal of Finance* 67 (6): 2341–2373.

Ghoshal, Sumantra, and Peter Moran. 1996. "Bad for Practice: A Critique of the Transaction Cost Theory." *Academy of Management Review* 21 (1): 13–47.

Gibbons, Robert. 2010. "Transaction-Cost Economics: Past, Present, and Future?" *Scandinavian Journal of Economics* 112 (2): 263–288.

Gil, Nuno. 2009. "Developing Cooperative Project Client-Supplier Relationships: How Much to Expect from Relational Contracts?" *California Management Review* 51 (2): 144–169.

Gompers, Paul, and Josh Lerner. 2000. "Money Chasing Deals? The Impact of Fund Inflows on Private Equity Valuation." *Journal of Financial Economics* 55 (2): 281–325.

Gramlich, Edward M. 1994. "Infrastructure Investment: A Review Essay." *Journal of Economic Literature* 32 (3): 1176–1196.

Granovetter, Mark S. 1973. "The Strength of Weak Ties." *American Journal of Sociology* 78 (6): 1360–1380.

———. 1985. “Economic Action and Social Structure: The Problem of Embeddedness.” *American Journal of Sociology* 91 (3): 481–510.

Granovetter, Mark S., and Richard Swedberg. 2001. *The Sociology of Economic Life*, Vol. 3. Boulder, CO: Westview Press.

Gudel, Paul J. 1998. “Relational Contract Theory and the Concept of Exchange.” *Buffalo Law Review* 46: 763.

Gulati, Ranjay, and Monica C. Higgins. 2003. “Which Ties Matter When? The Contingent Effects of Interorganizational Partnerships on IPO Success.” *Strategic Management Journal* 24 (2): 127–144.

Hachigian, Heather. 2014. “West Coast Infrastructure Exchange.” Case study, Carleton Centre for Community Innovation, Carleton University, Ottawa.

Hagermann, Lisa A., Gordon L. Clark, and Tessa Hebb. 2005. “Pension Funds and Urban Revitalization, New York Case Study: Competitive Returns and a Revitalized New York.” Working Papers in Employment, Work and Finance, Labor & Worklife Program, Harvard Law School, Cambridge, MA.

Haldane, Andrew G. 2010. “Patience and Finance.” Oxford China Business Forum Presentation, Beijing, September 9.

Harris, Robert S., Tim Jenkinson, and Steven N. Kaplan. 2014. “Private Equity Performance: What Do We Know?” *Journal of Finance* 69 (5): 1851–1882.

Henisz, Witold J., Raymond E. Levitt, and W. Richard Scott. 2012. “Toward a Unified Theory of Project Governance: Economic, Sociological and Psychological Supports for Relational Contracting.” *Engineering Project Organization Journal* 2 (1–2): 37–55.

HM Treasury. 2013. “Investing in Britain’s Future.” https://www.gov.uk/government/uploads/system/uploads/attachment_data/file/209279/PU1524_IUK_new_template.pdf.

Hochberg, Yael V., Alexander Ljungqvist, and Yang Lu. 2007. “Whom You Know Matters: Venture Capital Networks and Investment Performance.” *Journal of Finance* 62 (1): 251–301.

IFM. 2016. “IFM Investors.” https://www.ifminvestors.com.

IFSWF. 2016. “International Forum of Sovereign Wealth Funds.” http://www.ifswf.org.

Inderst, Georg. 2009. “Pension Fund Investment in Infrastructure.” OECD Working Papers on Insurance and Private Pensions no. 32, OECD, Paris.

Irving, Kym. 2009. “Overcoming Short-Termism: Mental Time Travel, Delayed Gratification and How Not to Discount the Future.” *Australian Accounting Review* 19 (4): 278–294.

Jackson, Matthew O. 2008. *Social and Economic Networks*. Princeton, NJ: Princeton University Press.

Jacobius, A. 2014. “OMERS Infrastructure Program Writes New Page in Investing.” *Pensions and Investments* 42 (18): 2.

Jenkinson, Tim, Howard Jones, and Jose Vicente Martinez. 2015. “Picking Winners? Investment Consultants’ Recommendations of Fund Managers.” *Journal of Finance* 71 (5): 2333–2370.

John, D. 2009. "The Fall and Fall of Babcock and Brown." *Sydney Morning Herald Business Day*, September 21.

Kaplan, Steven N., and Antoinette Schoar. 2005. "Private Equity Performance: Returns, Persistence, and Capital Flows." *Journal of Finance* 60 (4): 1791–1823.

Kay, John. 2012. "The Kay Review of UK Equity Markets and Long-Term Decision Making: Final Report, July 2012." *Applying Theory from Communication* 7 (8): 9–10.

Kimel, Dori. 2005. *From Promise to Contract: Towards a Liberal Theory of Contract.* London: Bloomsbury.

Knight, Eric R. W., and Rajiv Sharma. 2016. "Infrastructure as a Traded Product: A Relational Approach to Finance in Practice." *Journal of Economic Geography* 16 (4): 897–916.

Kogut, Bruce. 1988. "Joint Ventures: Theoretical and Empirical Perspectives." *Strategic Management Journal* 9 (4): 319–332.

Kortum, Samuel, and Josh Lerner. 2000. "Assessing the Contribution of Venture Capital to Innovation." *RAND Journal of Economics* 31 (4): 674–692.

Kvaløy, Ola, and Trond E. Olsen. 2005. "Endogenous Verifiability and Relational Contracting." *American Economic Review* 99 (5): 2193–2208.

Lagarde, C. 2011. "An Address to the 2011 International Finance Forum." November 9. http://www.imf.org/external/np/speeches/2011/110911.htm.

Lau, Sau-Him Paul, and Chor-Yiu Sin. 1997. "Public Infrastructure and Economic Growth: Time-Series Properties and Evidence." *Economic Record* 73 (221): 125–135.

Laverty, Kevin J. 1996. "Economic 'Short-Termism': The Debate, the Unresolved Issues, and the Implications for Management Practice and Research." *Academy of Management Review* 21 (3): 825–860.

Lee, Yikuan, and S. Tamer Cavusgil. 2006. "Enhancing Alliance Performance: The Effects of Contractual-Based versus Relational-Based Governance." *Journal of Business Research* 59 (8): 896–905.

Lerner, Joshua, Antoinette Schoar, and Wan Wongsunwai. 2007. "Smart Institutions, Foolish Choices: The Limited Partner Performance Puzzle." *Journal of Finance* 62 (2): 731–764.

Lerner, Joshua. 1994. "The Syndication of Venture Capital Investments." *Financial Management* 23 (3): 16–27.

Levin, Jonathan. 2003. "Relational Incentive Contracts." *American Economic Review* 93 (3): 835–857.

Lévi-Strauss, Claude. 1969. *The Elementary Structures of Kinship.* Boston: Beacon Press.

Lewis, Elizabeth. 2015. "A Bad Man's Guide to Private Equity and Pensions." Edmond J. Safra Working Papers no. 68, Harvard University, Cambridge, MA.

Ljungqvist, Alexander, and Matthew P. Richardson. 2003. "The Investment Behavior of Private Equity Fund Managers." NYU Working Paper no. S-FI-03-11, New York University.

LTIC. 2016. "Long-Term Investors Club." http://www.ltic.org.

Lucas, Robert E. 1988. "On the Mechanics of Economic Development." *Journal of Monetary Economics* 22 (1): 3–42.

Macaulay, Stewart. 1963. "Non-Contractual Relations in Business: A Preliminary Study." *American Sociological Review* 28 (1): 55–67.

MacIntosh, Jody, and Tom W. Scheibelhut. 2012. "How Large Pension Funds Organize Themselves: Findings from a Unique 19-fund Survey." *Rotman International Journal of Pension Management* 5 (1): 34.

Macneil, Ian R. 1974. "Restatement (Second) of Contracts and Presentation." *Virginia Law Review* (60): 589–610.

———. 1977. "Contracts: Adjustment of Long-Term Economic Relations under Classical, Neoclassical, and Relational Contract Law." *Northwestern University Law Review* 72: 854.

Malinowski, Bronislaw. 1922. "51. Kula; The Circulating Exchange of Valuables in the Archipelagoes of Eastern New Guinea." *Man* 20: 97–105.

Malkiel, Burton G. 2013. "Asset Management Fees and the Growth of Finance." *Journal of Economic Perspectives* 27 (2): 97–108.

Mayer, Kyle J., and Nicholas S. Argyres. 2004. "Learning to Contract: Evidence from the Personal Computer Industry." *Organization Science* 15 (4): 394–410.

McCahery, Joseph A., and Erik P. M. Vermeulen. 2008. "The Contractual Governance of Private Equity and Hedge Funds." Working paper, Tilburg University, Amsterdam.

Metrick, Andrew, and Ayako Yasuda. 2010. "The Economics of Private Equity Funds." *Review of Financial Studies* 23 (6): 2303–2341.

Meuleman, Miguel, Mike Wright, Sophie Manigart, and Andy Lockett. 2009. "Private Equity Syndication: Agency Costs, Reputation and Collaboration." *Journal of Business Finance & Accounting* 36 (5–6): 616–644.

Miller, Terrie, and Chris Flynn. 2010. "Internal Management Does Better after Costs." *CEM Insights* (October).

Mitsubishi Corporation. 2013. "Global Strategic Investment Alliance Announces Its First Investment." http://www.mitsubishicorp.com/jp/en/pr/archive/2013/html/0000021893.html.

Modigliani, Franco, and Merton H. Miller. 1958. "The Cost of Capital, Corporation Finance and the Theory of Investment." *American Economic Review* 48 (3): 261–297.

Molm, Linda D. 2007. "Power-Dependence Theory." In *The Blackwell Encyclopedia of Sociology*, edited by G. Ritzer. Malden, MA: Blackwell.

Monk, Ashby H. B., and R. Sharma. 2016. "'Organic Finance': The Incentives in Our Investment Products." Available at SSRN: http://ssrn.com/abstract=2696448.

Morley, A. W. 2002. "The Economic Benefits of Infrastructure Projects Procured with Private Finance." FIG XXII International Congress, Washington, DC, April 19–26.

Morrison, Alan D., and William J. Wilhelm Jr. 2007. *Investment banking: Institutions, Politics, and Law*, Vol. 10. Oxford: Oxford University Press.

Munnell, Alicia H. 1992. "Policy Watch: Infrastructure Investment and Economic Growth." *Journal of Economic Perspectives* 6 (4): 189–198.

Nahapiet, Janine, and Sumantra Ghoshal. 1998. "Social Capital, Intellectual Capital, and the Organizational Advantage." *Academy of Management Review* 23 (2): 242–266.

Nahapiet, Janine, Lynda Gratton, and Hector O. Rocha. 2005. "Knowledge and Relationships: When Cooperation Is the Norm." *European Management Review* 2 (1): 3–14.

NAPF. 2015. "National Association of Pension Funds." http://www.napf.co.uk.

Parkhe, Arvind, Stanley Wasserman, and David A. Ralston. 2006. "New Frontiers in Network Theory Development." *Academy of Management Review* 31 (3): 560–568.

Pfeffer, Jeffrey. 1972a. "Interorganizational Influence and Managerial Attitudes." *Academy of Management Journal* 15 (3): 317–330.

———. 1972b. "Merger as a Response to Organizational Interdependence." *Administrative Science Quarterly* 17 (3): 382–394.

———. 1972c. "Size and Composition of Corporate Boards of Directors: The Organization and Its Environment." *Administrative Science Quarterly* 17 (2): 218–228.

Pfeffer, Jeffrey, and Gerald R. Salancik. 2003. *The External Control of Organizations: A Resource Dependence Perspective.* Stanford, CA: Stanford University Press.

Phalippou, Ludovic, Christian Rauch, and Marc P. Umber. 2015. "Private Equity Portfolio Company Fees." Available at SSRN: http://ssrn.com/abstract=2702938.

PIP. 2016. "Pensions Infrastructure Platform." http://www.pipfunds.co.uk.

Podolny, Joel Marc. 2005. *Status Signals: A Sociological Study of Market Competition.* Princeton, NJ: Princeton University Press.

Polanyi, Michael. 1967. *The Tacit Dimension.* New York: Doubleday.

Poppo, Laura, and Todd Zenger. 2002. "Do Formal Contracts and Relational Governance Function as Substitutes or Complements?" *Strategic Management Journal* 23 (8): 707–725.

Porteous, David. 1999. "The Development of Financial Centres: Location, Information Externalities and Path Dependence." *Money and the Space Economy*: 95–114.

Powell, Walter W. 1998. "Learning from Collaboration: Knowledge and Networks in the Biotechnology and Pharmaceutical Industries." *California Management Review* 40 (3): 228–240.

PPF. 2009. "Pension Protection Fund." http://www.pensionprotectionfund.org.uk/About-Us/Pages/About-Us.aspx.

PPI. 2015. "Pacific Pensions Institute." http://www.ppi.institute/#home.

Preqin. 2013. Infrastructure Spotlight.

———. 2014a. Investor Outlook: Alternative Assets.

———. 2014b. "The State of Co-Investments: Preqin Private Equity Spotlight."

Probitas Partners. 2013. "Private Equity Institutional Investor Trends for 2014 Survey." http://probitaspartners.com/pdfs/probitas_private_equity_survey_trends2014.pdf.

Robinson, David T., and Berk A. Sensoy. 2013. "Do Private Equity Fund Managers Earn Their Fees? Compensation, Ownership, and Cash Flow Performance." *Review of Financial Studies* 26 (11): 2760–2797.

Romer, Paul M. 1986. "Increasing Returns and Long-Run Growth." *Journal of Political Economy* 94 (5): 1002–1037.

Rotter, Julian B. 1967. "A New Scale for the Measurement of Interpersonal Trust." *Journal of Personality* 35 (4): 651–665.

Sahlins, Marshall D. 1965a. *Essays in Economic Anthropology: Dedicated to the Memory of Karl Polany*. Seattle: University of Washington Press.

———. 1965b. "Exchange Value and the Diplomacy of Primitive Trade." In *Essays in Economic Anthropology: Dedicated to the Memory of Karl Polany*, 95–129. Seattle: University of Washington Press.

Sahlman, William A. 1990. "The Structure and Governance of Venture-Capital Organizations." *Journal of Financial Economics* 27 (2): 473–521.

Samila, Sampsa, and Olav Sorenson. 2011. "Venture Capital, Entrepreneurship, and Economic Growth." *Review of Economics and Statistics* 93 (1): 338–349.

Sarkar, P. 2013. "Canada Pension Plan Investment Board picks 80% in JV with Shapoorji Pallonji to Buy Office Buildings in India." VCCircle. http://www.vccircle.com/news/finance/2013/11/28/canada-pension-plan-investment-board-picks-80-jv-shapoorji-pallonji-buy.

Sarkar, Pooja, and P. R. Sanjai. 2014. "CPPIB Emerges as Largest Pension Fund Investor in India Infra Sector." http://www.livemint.com/Companies/lNKKfwEY20EDqPAlUlYqBJ/CPPIB-emerges-as-largest-pension-fund-investor-in-infra-sect.html.

Schakett, Tammy, Alan Flaschner, Tao Gao, and Adel El-Ansary. 2011. "Effects of Social Bonding in Business-to-Business Relationships." *Journal of Relationship Marketing* 10 (4): 264–280.

Shapoorji Pallonji. 2016. "Shapoorji Pallonji Engineering and Construction." http://www.shapoorji.in.

Sharma, Rajiv. 2012. "Infrastructure: An Emerging Asset Class for Institutional Investors." Conference on the Societal Function of Investment Asset Class: Implications for Responsible Investment, Harvard University, October.

———. 2013. "The Potential of Private Institutional Investors for Financing Transport Infrastructure." OECD ITF Discussion Paper.

Sharma, Rajiv, and Eric Knight. 2016. "The Role of Information Density in Infrastructure Investment." *Growth and Change* 47 (4): 520–534.

Sheffer, Dana A., and Raymond E. Levitt. 2010. "How Industry Structure Retards Diffusion of Innovations in Construction: Challenges and Opportunities." Working Paper no. 59, Collaboratory for Research on Global Projects, Stanford University, Stanford, CA.

Skyrms, Brian. 2004. *The Stag Hunt and the Evolution of Social Structure*. Cambridge: Cambridge University Press.

Smyth, Hedley. 2014. *Relationship Management and the Management of Projects*. Abingdon, UK: Routledge.

Solow, Robert M. 1956. "A Contribution to the Theory of Economic Growth." *Quarterly Journal of Economics* 70 (1): 65–94.

Steindl, Martin. 2013. "The Alignment of Interests between the General and the Limited Partner in a Private Equity Fund—the Ultimate Governance Nut to Crack?" Harvard Law School Forum on Corporate Governance and Financial Regulation.

Stone, Richard. 2005. *The Modern Law of Contract.* N.p.: Psychology Press.

Stoughton, Neal M., Youchang Wu, and Josef Zechner. 2011. "Intermediated Investment Management." *Journal of Finance* 66 (3): 947–980.

Stuart, Toby E., Ha Hoang, and Ralph C. Hybels. 1999. "Interorganizational Endorsements and the Performance of Entrepreneurial Ventures." *Administrative Science Quarterly* 44 (2): 315–349.

Stucke, Rüdiger. 2011. "Updating History." Available at SSRN: http://ssrn.com/abstract=1967636.

Swedberg, Richard. 2000. *Max Weber and the Idea of Economic Sociology.* Princeton, NJ: Princeton University Press.

Swensen, David F. 2009. *Pioneering Portfolio Management: An Unconventional Approach to Institutional Investment, Fully Revised and Updated.* New York: Simon and Schuster.

TIAA-CREF. 2012. "Investing in Agriculture." In *TIAA-CREF Private Markets Asset Management.* https://www.tiaa.org/public/pdf/C11718_Agriculture+Primer_Dec+2013.pdf.

Timmons, Jeffry A., and William D. Bygrave. 1986. "Venture Capital's Role in Financing Innovation for Economic Growth." *Journal of Business Venturing* 1 (2): 161–176.

Torrance, Morag I. 2007. "The Power of Governance in Financial Relationships: Governing Tensions in Exotic Infrastructure Territory." *Growth and Change* 38 (4): 671–695.

———. 2009. "The Rise of a Global Infrastructure Market through Relational Investing." *Economic Geography* 85 (1): 75–97.

Towers Watson. 2015a. Global Alternatives Survey.

———. 2015b. "Global Pension Assets Study."

United Nations. 2008. "Transnational Corporations and the Infrastructure Challenge." *World Investment Report.* http://unctad.org/en/Docs/wir2008_en.pdf.

Uzzi, Brian. 1997. "Social Structure and Competition in Interfirm Networks: The Paradox of Embeddedness." *Administrative Science Quarterly* 42 (1): 35–67.

Vargo, Stephen L., and Robert F. Lusch. 2004. "Evolving to a New Dominant Logic for Marketing." *Journal of Marketing* 68 (1): 1–17.

Warren, Geoff. 2014. "Long-Term Investing: What Determines Investment Horizon?" CIFR Paper no. 39, Centre for International Finance and Regulation, Sydney.

Watson Wyatt. 2009. "Improving Fees in Infrastructure." October.

Weber, Max. 1978. *Economy and Society: An Outline of Interpretive Sociology.* Berkeley: University of California Press.

WEF. 2011. "The Future of Long-Term Investing." World Economic Forum. http://www3.weforum.org/docs/WEF_FutureLongTermInvesting_Report_2011.pdf.

———. 2014. "Direct Investing by Institutional Investors: Implications for Investors and Policy-Makers. World Economic Forum." http://www3.weforum.org/docs/WEFUSA_DirectInvestingInstitutionalInvestors.pdf.

Williamson, Oliver E. 1979. "Transaction-Cost Economics: The Governance of Contractual Relations." *Journal of Law & Economics* 22 (2): 233–261.

———. 1985. *The Economic Institutions of Capitalism: Firms, Markets, Relational Contracting.* New York: Free Press.

Wilson, Robert. 1968. "The Theory of Syndicates." *Econometrica: Journal of the Econometric Society* 36 (1): 119–132.

World Bank. 2015. "Institutional Investors: The Unfulfilled $100 Trillion Promise." http://www.worldbank.org/en/news/feature/2015/06/18/institutional-investors-the-unfulfilled-100-trillion-promise.

Yamagishi, Toshio, and Karen S. Cook. 1993. "Generalized Exchange and Social Dilemmas." *Social Psychology Quarterly* 56 (4): 235–248.

Zaheer, Akbar, Remzi Gözübüyük, and Hana Milanov. 2010. "It's the Connections: The Network Perspective in Interorganizational Research." *Academy of Management Perspectives* 24 (1): 62–77.

Index

Page numbers followed by "f" or "t" indicate material in figures or tables.

About the Authors

ASHBY MONK is Executive and Research Director of Stanford University's Global Projects Center.

RAJIV SHARMA is Research Director at Stanford's Global Projects Center and Honorary Research Associate at Oxford University's Smith School of Enterprise and the Environment.

DUNCAN L. SINCLAIR is Vice Chair at Deloitte.